Introduction

In 1945 the Soviet aircraft industry began a large-scale effort to create jet-powered aircraft, trying to catch up with the progress made in this field abroad. The work centred on two main areas – aerodynamics and propulsion; the first Soviet attempts to create a turbojet engine had been undertaken back in 1942 by Arkhip Mikhaïlovich Lyul'ka. After the Second World War aviation technology was taken up to a qualitatively new level. The advent of turbojet engines expanded the speed envelope of aircraft, making supersonic flight a distinct possibility. However, as aircraft approached transonic speeds equivalent to Mach 0.8-1.1, unusual and dangerous phenomena (later called the 'wave crisis') set in, jeopardising flight safety. On some parts of the airframe the airflow reached the speed of sound, departing as it did; the airflow pattern and pressure distribution over the airframe changed, causing a sharp increase in drag at transonic speeds, as well as a reduction in

wing lift and a deterioration of stability and controllability. This combination of unwelcome phenomena came to be known as the 'sound barrier'.

Fundamental research showed that the 'sound barrier' problem could be overcome by using swept-back wings and tail surfaces. Yet even early tests of wind tunnel models with swept wings at transonic speeds conducted by the Central Aerodynamics & Hydrodynamics Institute named after Nikolay Ye. Zhukovskiy (TsAGI – *Tsentrahl'nyy aero- i ghidrodinamicheskiy institoot*) revealed that a range of specific problems needed to be addressed before such wings could find use on actual aircraft. These problems included airflow departure at high angles of attack, spanwise airflow from root to tip (which increased drag), and the decrease of lift at the tips combined with the increase of lift at the roots (tip stall), which resulted in the aircraft's tendency to drop a wing.

In 1946 TsAGI began large-scale research into the aerodynamics of swept wings and control authority, working in close cooperation with several Soviet aircraft design bureaux. These included OKB-301 headed by Semyon Alekseyevich Lavochkin, which had achieved fame as a 'fighter maker' during the Great Patriotic War of 1941-45 by developing such aircraft as the La-5 and La-7. (OKB = *opytno-konstrooktorskoye byuro* – experimental design bureau; the number is a code allocated for security reasons.) Research conducted in 1947-48 involved wind tunnel tests both of isolated wings or control surfaces and of complete aircraft models. These tests yielded valuable theoretical data and practical results associated with the use of swept wings. In particular, new wing airfoils were developed; the stability and handling problems peculiar to swept-wing aircraft were solved to some extent. Recommendations were issued for installing boundary layer

Brothers-in-arms – and competitors. Left to right: Semyon Alekseyevich Lavochkin, Aleksandr Sergeyevich Yakovlev and Artyom Ivanovich Mikoyan, the Chief Designers of the OKB-301, OKB-115 and OKB-155 design bureaux respectively that were the Soviet Union's main 'fighter makers' at the time.

Above: A production '150' (La-150) fighter serialled '21 Red'. Note the nose-up ground angle, the high-set stabilisers and the badge of the Gor'kiy aircraft factory No.21 on the nose.

Above: '52 Red', the '152' (La-152) development aircraft powered by an RD-10 turbojet, also had a 'tadpole' (pod-and-boom) layout but featured mid-set wings. Note the lateral position of the cannons.

The '156' (La-156), a testbed for the RD-10F afterburning turbojet The nose gear unit turned through 90° during retraction to lie flat under the engine, hence the unusually large nosewheel well doors.

fences on the wing upper surface to limit spanwise airflow, and the wings' aerodynamic parameters required for a given design Mach number were defined.

The Soviet aero engine designers lost no time either. Considering that the first indigenous turbojet engines were still at an early development phase and could not be used safely, the Soviet aircraft industry chose to reverse-engineer two German axial-flow turbojets that had fallen into Soviet hands at the end of the war. The Junkers Jumo 004B rated at 900 kgp (1,980 lbst) for take-off was built in the Soviet Union as the RD-10 (*reaktivnyy dvigatel'* – jet engine), while the 800-kgp (1,760-

lbst) BMW 003A was produced as the RD-20. These engines powered the first Soviet jet fighter types – the Mikoyan/Gurevich MiG-9, the Yakovlev Yak-15, the Lavochkin 'aircraft 150' (La-150) and the Sukhoi Su-9 (the first to be thus designated; in-house code *izdeliye* K) which are described in detail in Red Star Vol.4. (*Izdeliye* [product] such-and-such was, and still is, a common way of coding Soviet/Russian military hardware items in OKB or factory documents for security reasons. The designation Su-9 was re-used much later for a totally different aircraft known in-house as the T-43.) Yet as early as 1946 it was clear that the German booty engines had

reached their limit and were no good as a powerplant for a truly modern fighter by the day's standards. Since state-of-the-art Soviet engines with the required thrust rating were still unavailable (developing them turned out to be a protracted affair), the Soviet Ministry of Aircraft Industry (MAP – *Ministerstvo aviatsionnoy promyshlennosti*) looked abroad once again for a suitable powerplant.

After the Second World War Great Britain emerged as the leader in jet propulsion technology development. Hence in late 1946 a Soviet delegation comprising Chief Designer Artyom I. Mikoyan (head of the OKB-155 fighter design bureau), Chief Designer Vladimir Ya. Klimov (head of the OKB-117 engine design bureau) and Professor S. T. Kishkin (a notable specialist in aviation structural materials) visited the UK. The delegation succeeded in obtaining the latest centrifugal-flow turbojets developed by Rolls-Royce – the Nene I and Nene II (the latter version was rated at 2,270 kgp/5,000 lbst) and the 1,590-lbst (3,500-lbst) Derwent V. Apart from the adequate thrust rating, these engines boasted a long time between overhauls (TBO) of 180 hours; in contrast, the initial TBO of the RD-10 and RD-20 was a mere 25 hours. The acquisition of the British turbojets gave a powerful impetus to Soviet jet engine and jet aircraft development. Again, it was decided to copy the Nene and Derwent, putting them into production urgently as the RD-45 and RD-500 respectively. (In these cases, 45 and 500 were the numbers of the MAP plants earmarked for manufacturing these engines.) Soviet aircraft design bureaux were now tasked with developing new combat aircraft prototypes designed around these engines. Thus was born the second generation of Soviet jet tactical fighters.

On 11th March 1947 the Central Committee of the Soviet Union's Communist Party and the Soviet Council of Ministers issued a joint directive to this effect. The directive specified the key performance figures of the future fighters, including a top speed of some 1,000-1,200 km/h (621-633 mph), a service ceiling of 13,000 m (42,650 ft) and a normal range of 1,200 km (745 miles) at 10,000 m (32,810 ft) on internal fuel, increasing to 1,600 km (993 miles) with drop tanks. The Soviet Air Force (VVS – *Voyenno-vozdooshnyye seely*) demanded that the fighter should be armed with at least three cannons of 23-mm (.90) or heavier calibre. Other mandatory design features included airbrakes and a pressurised cockpit, since the new fighters were supposed to operate at altitudes in excess of 10,000 m (32,810 ft) where flying and fighting with just an ordinary oxygen mask was out of the question. Pursuant to the said directive the prototype fighters were to be submitted for state acceptance trials in December 1947.

Lavochkin's Last Jets

Yefim Gordon

Original translation by Dmitriy Komissarov

MIDLAND
An imprint of
Ian Allan Publishing

Lavochkin's Last Jets
© 2007 Yefim Gordon

ISBN (10) 1 85780 253 5
ISBN (13) 978 1 85780 253 5

Published by Midland Publishing
4 Watling Drive, Hinckley, LE10 3EY, England
Tel: 01455 254 490 Fax: 01455 254 495
E-mail: midlandbooks@compuserve.com

Midland Publishing is an imprint of
Ian Allan Publishing Ltd

Worldwide distribution (except North America):
Midland Counties Publications
4 Watling Drive, Hinckley, LE10 3EY, England
Telephone: 01455 254 450 Fax: 01455 233 737
E-mail: midlandbooks@compuserve.com
www.midlandcountiessuperstore.com

North American trade distribution:
Specialty Press Publishers & Wholesalers Inc.
39966 Grand Avenue, North Branch, MN 55056, USA
Tel: 651 277 1400 Fax: 651 277 1203
Toll free telephone: 800 895 4585
www.specialtypress.com

Design concept and layout by
Polygon Press Ltd (Moscow, Russia)
Line drawings by NPO Lavochkin, Andrey
Yurgenson and the late Ivnamin Sultanov
Colour artwork by Andrey Yurgenson

This book is illustrated with photos by Yefim
Gordon, Tony Buttler, as well as from the Central
State Archive of the National Economy, the archives
of NPO Lavochkin, Ghennadiy Serov, Yefim
Gordon, Sergey and Dmitriy Komissarov, *Jane's All
the World's Aircraft*, *Samolyoty Mira* magazine and
the Russian Aviation Research Trust

Printed in England by Ian Allan Printing Ltd
Riverdene Business Park, Molesey Road,
Hersham, Surrey, KT12 4RG

Visit the Ian Allan Publishing website at:
www.ianallanpublishing.com

Contents

Title page: A pair of red-nosed La-15s of the 196th Fighter Regiment takes off from Kubinka AB.
This page: A retouched photo of the 'aircraft 168' prototype from a test report. Note the long ventral strake of increased area (compare this with the photos in Chapter 2).

Front cover: The '200' (La-200) interceptor in its original configuration with a centrebody radome and twin mainwheels.
Rear cover: La-15 '01 Red' in the Central Russian Air Force Museum in Monino.

The famous aircraft designer Aleksandr S. Yakovlev, head of the OKB-115 design bureau, chose the line of the least resistance. Taking his second jet fighter (the Yak-17) as the starting point, he used the same 'tadpole' (pod-and-boom) layout with a forward-mounted engine exhausting under the fuselage for his first aircraft powered by the new RR Derwent V – the Yak-23 light fighter. Like its predecessor, the machine had thick unswept wings and lacked cockpit pressurisation, while the armament was limited to two 23-mm cannons and the fuel load was also extremely limited in order to save weight. This allowed OKB-115 to build and test the Yak-23 prototypes within an incredibly short time span; the aircraft was submitted to the Red Banner State Research Institute of the Soviet Air Force (GK NII VVS – *Gosoodarstvennyy krasnoznamyonnyy naoochno-issledovatel'-skiy institoot Voyenno-vozdooshnykh seel*) for state acceptance trials as early as 22nd October 1947. True, the 'quick fix' approach did not allow high performance to be attained; the Yak-23's maximum speed recorded during the trials was only 925 km/h (574 mph) and many other requirements of the Air Force were not met. Nevertheless, the 'first past the post' principle worked – the Yak-23 was cleared for production and service, being a more advanced fighter than the MiG-9 and Yak-17 then in production.

Still, the military and the MAP top brass were not satisfied with this state of affairs, demanding the development of higher-performance combat jets. Soon the Soviet Union's four principal 'fighter makers' – Artyom I. Mikoyan's OKB-155, Aleksandr S. Yakovlev's OKB-115, Semyon A. Lavochkin's OKB-301 and Pavel O. Sukhoi's OKB-134 –

Above: Aero engine designer Vladimir Ya. Klimov (left) and Artyom I. Mikoyan examine a Gloster Meteor fighter at a British airfield.

were pitted against each other in a competition for the Soviet Air Force's new jet fighter.

The abovementioned Vol.4 in this series gave a description of the Lavochkin OKB's early jets – the '150', '152', '156' and '174TK' experimental fighters, while the very last aircraft from the Lavochkin stable – the '250' experimental heavy interceptor (aka La-250, or Anaconda) – was dealt with in Red Star Vol.19. This book describes the remaining jet fighters created by OKB-301 in the late 1940s and early 1950s.

The Yak-23 was the first Soviet fighter to be powered by the Rolls-Royce Derwent V (RD-500) engine. One of the prototypes serialled '52 Yellow' is shown here.

Above: The Rolls-Royce Nene centrifugal-flow turbojet suspended from an overhead bearer. Note the sectioned wire mesh screen protecting the inlet and the lateral mounting lugs on the compressor casing just ahead of the combustion chambers. The Nene I and II were built in the Soviet Union as the RD-45.

The Rolls-Royce Derwent V was a smaller engine utilising the same layout. It was likewise copied in the USSR and built as the RD-500.

Chapter 1

'Little Arrow'

'Aircraft 160' (La-160) Experimental Fighter (second use of designation)

In December 1946 Semyon A. Lavochkin's OKB-301 started work on the Soviet Union's first swept-wing jet fighter. As noted in the introductory section, this work proceeded in close cooperation with TsAGI, the nation's leading research establishment in the field of aviation.

The objective of attaining, and ultimately exceeding, the speed of sound required the fighter to utilise a completely new layout; first and foremost this concerned the wing design. TsAGI's most prominent scientists, assisted by the Lavochkin OKB's designers, racked their brains in an effort to find a solution. Large-scale research, including numerous wind tunnel tests and experiments, showed clearly that reaching the required speeds and breaking the sound barrier was only possible on a swept-wing aircraft. The swept wings delayed the onset of the 'wave crisis' until higher speeds and alleviated the abrupt nature of its onset. At the same time the researchers and designers took on the issues of ensuring adequate stability of a swept-wing aircraft at high AoAs, ensuring structural integrity of the swept wings and so on.

Officially the new fighter was designated 'aircraft 160' (or simply '160'), although some publications refer to it as the La-160. (The 'La' prefix denoting the manufacturer was normally used for aircraft that had been cleared for production and service.) At the Lavochkin OKB, however, the aircraft was dubbed **Strelka** (in the literal meaning, 'little arrow') as a reference to the swept wings (*strelovidnoye krylo* – lit. 'arrow-shaped wings'). The aircraft

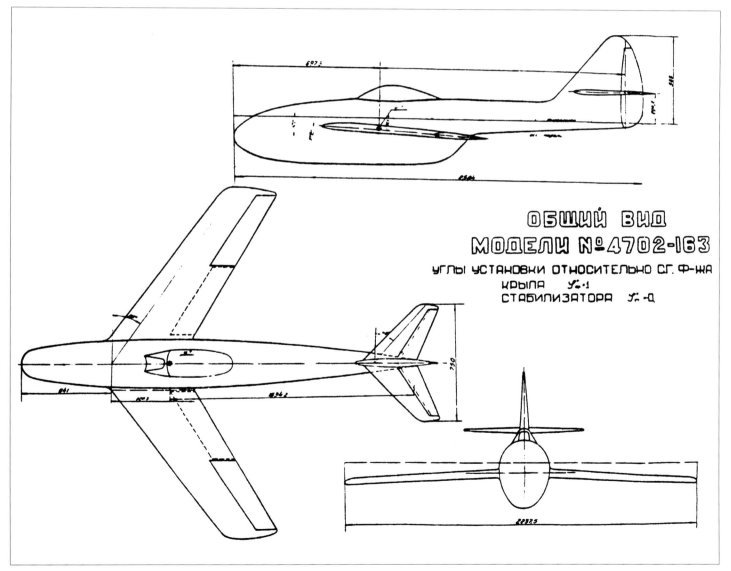

A three-view of a wind tunnel model designated No.4702-163 and representing the 'aircraft 160' experimental fighter. The wing and stabiliser incidence is 1° and 0° respectively. The conventional vertical tail made a striking contrast with the swept tailplane. The air intake and engine nozzle are omitted.

The same model in the TsAGI wind tunnel, seen from below (the 'step' of the engine nozzle is clearly visible). Note that the wings were placed well forward on the fuselage.

was an all-metal mid-wing monoplane with wings swept back 35° at quarter-chord; the wing area was 15.9 m² (170.96 sq ft). The wings made use of high-speed airfoils developed by TsAGI and were fitted with boundary layer fences limiting spanwise airflow (two on each side). Wind tunnel tests had shown that the fences delayed the onset of tip stall at high angles of attack during vigorous manoeuvres (typically during a dogfight) and in take-off/landing mode; this made for adequate stability and control at high AoAs. For the first time in Soviet aircraft design practice, the most highly stressed elements of the structure were made of the new V95 high-strength aluminium alloy.

Here it should be noted that in April 1945 OKB-301 had two fighter projects running in parallel – the single-engined '150' light fighter and the twin-engined '160' heavy fighter. The latter – the first aircraft to bear this designation – was a totally different aircraft from the one described here, featuring unswept wings and two Jumo 004B engines. However, working

on two jet fighter projects at once would have stretched the Lavochkin OKB's resources too far, large though the design team was. Chief Designer Semyon A. Lavochkin acted wisely in this situation: using the fact that his aide Semyon M. Alekseyev (who was responsible for the '160') had been appointed Chief Designer of OKB-21 in Gor'kiy (at Lavochkin's recommendation, mind you), he put the '160' project on hold, allowing the design team to concentrate on the other aircraft. (OKB-21 was the design office of MAP's aircraft factory No.21 named after Sergo Ordzhonikidze in Gor'kiy. The city has now been renamed back to Nizhniy Novgorod, while the plant itself is known as the 'Sokol' (= Falcon) Nizhniy Novgorod Aircraft Factory.) Not to be outdone, Alekseyev started work on a series of his own projects, including the I-211 and I-215 twinjet fighters, after arriving in Gor'kiy; see Red Star Volume 4.

Given the unavailability of more powerful engines, OKB-301 had no choice but to use the *izdeliye* YuF afterburning turbojet (some-

times called RD-10F) – a derivative of the Junkers Jumo 004B, which was referred to in Soviet documents as *izdeliye* Yu. (This was the last-but-one letter of the Cyrillic alphabet and the phonetic rendering of the 'Ju for Junkers' prefix. YuF stood for *Yumo, forseerovannyy* – Jumo, uprated.) The new version with an afterburning thrust of some 1,140 kgp (2,510 lbst) had been developed in-house by plant No.301 where the Lavochkin OKB had its premises. The standard RD-10 (*izdeliye* Yu) was obviously too small an engine to allow the Air Force's performance target to be met. As related in Red Star Vol.4, several Soviet aircraft designers had reached this conclusion; now, assisted actively by the Central Aero Engine Institute (TsIAM – *Tsentrahl'nyy institoot aviatsionnovo motorostroyeniya*), the Yakovlev and Sukhoi OKBs also attempted to uprate the RD-10 in house. At the Lavochkin OKB the task was assigned to Ivan A. Merkoolov, a well-known designer of ramjet engines who had joined OKB-301 with his team in April 1945.

In 1946 the special design section of plant No.301 consecutively developed two afterburners for the RD-10. The initial version retained the baseline engine's variable nozzle whose area was adjusted by a translating cone (centrebody) according to engine rpm; quite simply, five additional combustion chambers were fitted downstream of the original nozzle. Bench tests showed that the maximum thrust increased by 31.9%; however, cooling problems arose with the centrebody and the afterburner combustion chambers. Therefore the original design was scrapped in favour of a so-called dual-action nozzle featuring a single annular afterburner combustion chamber with a burner ring. The translating cone gave place to movable petals adjusting the nozzle area; their position was controlled by the existing nozzle regulator coupled with an afterburner fuel feed cock. A second fuel pump catering for the afterburner was added to the engine's accessory gearbox. Thus, the cooling problem had been resolved by placing the engine parts outside the hottest exhaust gas stream; also, the redesigned version was simpler and lighter. Unlike the Yakovlev OKB's afterburning version of the RD-10 (confusingly, likewise referred to as the RD-10F), which had a long afterburner assembly, the Lavochkin version had almost identical dimensions to the standard non-afterburning engine; it was only 100 mm (3¹⁵⁄₁₆ in) longer and 31 kg (68 lb) heavier. Less DC generator and hydraulic pump the *izdeliye* YuF was 4.0355 m (13 ft 2⅞ in) long, with a diameter of 0.83 m (2 ft 8⁴³⁄₆₄ in), and had a dry weight of 761 kg (1,677 lb).

On several occasions the engine delivered a static thrust of up to 1,240 kgp (2,730 lbst) in afterburner mode – an improvement of 340 kgp (750 lbst) or more than 30% over the standard RD-10; the thrust loss in dry mode did not exceed 30 kgp (66 lbst). The modification had no adverse effect on the engine's TBO. Other contemporary documents give somewhat lower thrust figures for the Lavochkin OKB's version ranging from 1,140 to 1,050-1,100 kgp (from 2,510 to 2,315-2,425 lbst) in afterburner mode. Thus, the engineers obtained a considerably higher thrust while retaining the engine's cross-section area and basic dimensions.

By 6th November 1946 the Lavochkin OKB's RD-10F engine (*izdeliye* YuF) had successfully completed a 25-hour bench test cycle in the propulsion laboratory of plant No.301. The event was probably timed to a major state holiday – the anniversary of the October Revolution, which was celebrated on 7th November. In the spring of 1947 the engine was flight-tested in a purpose-built development aircraft known at the OKB as 'aircraft 156' (see photo on page 4).

The chosen powerplant dictated the fighter's layout. As already mentioned, the swept wings were mid-set; the tail surfaces were also swept back. The engine was housed in the centre fuselage, breathing through a nose air intake; because the hot afterburner section required intensive cooling, the aft extremity of the fuselage was cut away so that the afterburner was exposed to the slipstream. A heat shield protected the rear fuselage underside. The aircraft had a tricycle landing gear, all three units retracting into the fuselage; hence the wheel track was quite narrow. The pilot was provided with an ejection seat. The armament consisted of two 37-mm (1.45 calibre) cannons. 'Aircraft 160' had an empty weight of 2,738 kg (6,036 lb) and a take-off weight of 4,060 kg (8,950 lb).

The prototype was completed in July 1947. The Lavochkin OKB's chief test pilot Ivan Ye. Fyodorov was appointed the machine's project test pilot, performing the maiden flight successfully on 23rd July. Three days later the '160' commenced a special trials programme held jointly by the OKB and the Flight Research Institute named after Mikhail M. Gromov (LII – *Lyotno-issledovatel'skiy institoot*). Since the afterburning engine had a very limited service life, the main thrust (no pun intended) of the test programme was directed at establishing the fighter's stability and handling at high transonic speeds. In August-November 1947 the prototype made a total of 25 test flights. The thrust of the RD-10F proved to be inadequate, so the performance parameters and handling were explored in a shallow dive. Gradually expanding the fighter's speed envelope, Fyodorov attained a maximum speed of 1,050 km/h (652 mph) at 5,700 m (18,700 ft) in one

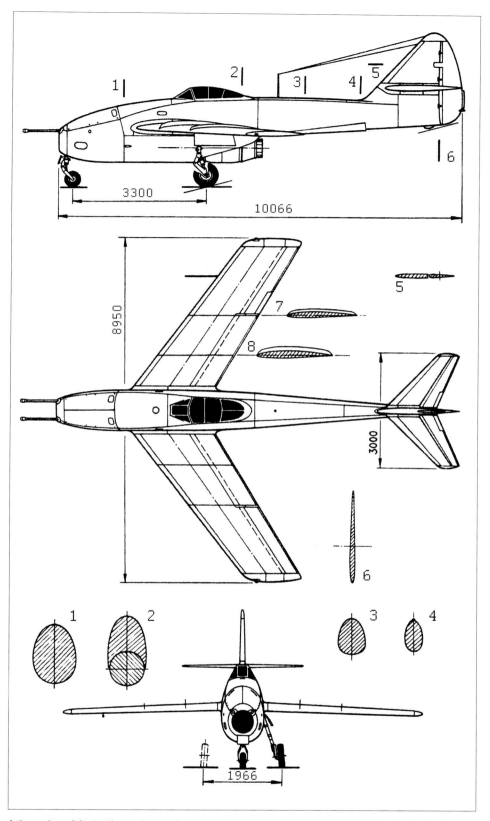

A three-view of the '160' experimental fighter, showing the exposed afterburner section and the heat shield aft of it. Note the placement of the cannons and their protruding barrels.

of the flights; this amounted to Mach 0.92 – that is, just 8% short of the speed of sound. The fighter handled well at this speed and there were no apparent obstacles to flying even faster.

On 19th November the '160' completed the joint test programme; now it was time to transfer the machine to GK NII VVS for state acceptance trials. The speeds attained so far confirmed the results of the wind tunnel

Above: The '160' was rolled out minus cannon armament, as shown here. This photo was taken from a high point in order to show clearly the wing and stabiliser sweepback. Note that the inboard and outboard wing fences have different height.

A head-on view of the '160' accentuating the wing position and the narrow track of the tall main gear units.; the aircraft must have been pretty scary to land. Note that the cannons have now been fitted.

Above: Another view of the '160' during manufacturer's flight tests. The paintwork appears to have a differing degree of gloss on different parts of the airframe, but this is probably a trick of the light.

This side view emphasises the wing sweep, as well as the length of the cannon barrels. Note the engine afterburner section exposed for better cooling and the transverse frame members on the sliding canopy section.

Lavochkin OKB chief test pilot Ivan Yevgrafovich Fyodorov, shown here with his many orders and medals earned in the war, test-flew the '160'.

tests, proving that the previous research had been in the right direction. This programme had a major effect on the subsequent development of fast jets in the Soviet Union.

Interestingly, in 1946-47 the Soviet Union went to great lengths to keep up with the West in jet aircraft technology, and the Soviet aircraft industry (and some other industries as well) spared no efforts to achieve this goal. Apart from the actual construction of viable jet aircraft, demonstrating the Soviet achievements in this field for the world to see was an important objective at the time. Thus, in the spring of 1947 the then Minister of Aircraft Industry Aleksey I. Shakhoorin issued an order requiring all of the nation's leading aircraft design bureaus to complete and test prototypes of new models of aircraft in time for the traditional Aviation Day flypast at Moscow's Tushino airfield. Specifically, OKB-301 was required to complete construction of the 'aircraft 160' swept-wing fighter powered by the afterburning version of the RD-10 turbojet by 20th June and complete initial flight tests of this aircraft by 25th July, among other things. Two alternative dates were set for the flypast (3rd August and 18th August). In the latter case, the 53 development aircraft representing 20 assorted types (as envisaged by the flying display programme) would be augmented by three more aircraft – Lavochkin's 'aircraft 160', the Alekseyev I-211 straight-wing twin-turbojet fighter with a pressurised cockpit and the prototype of the Yakovlev Yak-16 twin-engined short-haul airliner.

The parade eventually took place on 3rd August 1947, but the '160' was included all right. The long line-astern formation was headed by test pilot Sergey N. Anokhin flying the Yak-19 experimental fighter, followed by G. S. Klimushkin in the Yak-15U and Mikhail I. Ivanov in the Yak-23. Next came a gaggle of Lavochkin prototypes – the '150' flown by Stepan P. Sooproon, the '156' flown by S. F. Mashkovskiy, the '160' flown by Ivan Ye. Fyodorov; then a MiG-9 piloted by A. I. Chernoboorov, the Su-9 (izdeliye K) flown by Andrey G. Kochetkov and its derivative, the Su-11 (izdeliye LK) flown by Gheorgiy M. Shiyanov. The fast jets were followed by the piston-engined Il'yushin IL-18 long-haul airliner (the first aircraft to bear this designation) with the Kokkinaki brothers (Vladimir and Konstantin) at the controls. Next came the Tupolev Tu-10 experimental bomber flown by A. D. Perelyot. The cherry on the cake was a V formation of three Tupolev B-4 (Tu-4) heavy bombers captained by N. S. Rybko, Mark L. Gallai and A. G. Vasil'chenko.

Although it went down in Soviet/Russian aviation history as the first indigenous swept-wing aircraft and a harbinger of supersonic speeds, the '160' had an unhappy fate. The aircraft broke up in mid-air during a test flight with the objective of establishing the machine's maximum speed; the structural failure was caused by violent wing vibration. The crash reinforced the position of the sceptics who did not believe in swept wings. Indeed, many of the Soviet aircraft designers were wary of swept wings after this accident and opted for 'good old' unswept wings when tasked with developing the second generation of jet fighters. Some OKBs went so far as to develop straight-wing versions of new swept-wing designs in parallel as an 'insurance policy' in case the baseline swept-wing version went wrong. One can hardly blame them for being 'over-cautious'; wings with sweep angles in excess of 20° were not yet adequately studied at the time and the designers were breaking new ground. Swept-wing aircraft were characterised by unusually high landing speeds, which necessitated new piloting techniques. Also, from a structural standpoint the swept wings were something of a liability, being heavier than unswept wings having the same area and aspect ratio. Small wonder the designers were playing safe.

Still, new technology won. Shortly afterwards the Lavochkin, Mikoyan, Yakovlev and Sukhoi OKBs and other Soviet design bureaux began testing swept-wing aircraft fitted with more powerful turbine engines. Offering much higher speed, the swept-wing aircraft and jet engines quickly displaced the hitherto traditional straight-wing aircraft and piston engines to very secondary roles.

If the 'aircraft 160' had its moment of glory, so did the people who designed and flew it. In 1947 Chief Designer Semyon A. Lavochkin was awarded the prestigious Stalin Prize for creating the '160' fighter, while test pilot Ivan Ye. Fyodorov received the even more prestigious Hero of the Soviet Union (HSU) title for testing the machine.

Basic specifications of the 'aircraft 160' fighter

Powerplant	1 x RD-10F (izdeliye YuF)
Afterburning thrust, kgp (lbst)	1,140 (2,510)
Length overall	10.06 m (33 ft 0 in)
Height on ground	4.125 m (13 ft 6¹³⁄₃₂ in)
Wing span	8.95 m (29 ft 4²³⁄₆₄ in)
Stabiliser span	3.0 m (9 ft 10⁷⁄₆₄ in)
Wing area, m² (sq ft)	15.9 (170.96)
Landing gear track	1.96 m (6 ft 5¹¹⁄₆₄ in)
Landing gear wheelbase	3.3 m (10 ft 9⁵⁹⁄₆₄ in)
Wing sweep at quarter-chord	35°
Stabiliser sweep at quarter-chord	40°
Empty weight, kg (lb)	2,738 (6,036)
Take-off weight, kg (lb)	4,060 (8,950)
Fuel capacity, litres (Imp gal)	1,080 (237.6)
Maximum Mach number attained	0.92
Estimated maximum speed in level flight at 5,000 m (16,400 ft), km/h (mph)	970 (602)
Maximum speed in a dive at 5,700 m (18,700 ft), km/h (mph)	1,050 (652)
Estimated climb time to 5,000 m, minutes	4.2
Estimated service ceiling, m (ft)	12,200 (40,030)
Estimated range at 10,000 m (32,810 ft), km (miles)	1,000 (621)
Armament	2 x 37-mm cannons

Chapter 2

Chasing Mach 1

'Aircraft 168' (La-168) Experimental Fighter

In parallel with the 'aircraft 160', in December 1946 OKB-301 began development of another swept-wing jet fighter, and a very different one at that. Designated 'aircraft 168', this fighter represented a departure from the pod-and-boom layout that was characteristic of earlier Lavochkin jets. The fighter had a cigar-shaped fuselage with the cockpit located ahead of the wings and the engine buried in the rear fuselage so that the nozzle was located at its aft extremity. The wings, featuring 37°20' sweep at quarter-chord, were shoulder-mounted and had marked anhedral (4°30'); the latter feature was intended to enhance the fighter's manoeuvrability by eliminating excessive lateral stability. The

swept tail surfaces were also new, featuring a cruciform layout with the horizontal tail set high up on the fin – in fact, it was almost a T-tail. The chosen layout allowed the fighter to attain high transonic speeds, despite the rather modest thrust available.

Speaking of thrust, the aircraft was built around a Rolls-Royce Nene II turbojet delivering 2,270 kgp (5,000 lbst) for take-off; this would give the fighter a higher thrust/weight ratio and ensure much higher performance as compared to the then-current fighters powered by the smaller turbojets of German origin. As already mentioned, the engine was housed in the rear fuselage, breathing through a circular air intake in the extreme

nose; the intake was divided by a splitter into two elliptical-section inlet ducts that flanked the cockpit and avionics/equipment bays to merge ahead of the engine. The monocoque fuselage was built in two sections; the rear fuselage complete with the tail unit could be detached and wheeled away on a dolly, exposing the engine completely for maintenance or removal.

For the first time on a Lavochkin aircraft, the '168' had a pressurised cockpit equipped with a new, more capable ejection seat. Another 'first' for OKB-301 was the use of two airbrakes installed on the rear fuselage sides. The tricycle landing gear retracted into the fuselage, the nosewheel retracting aft and the

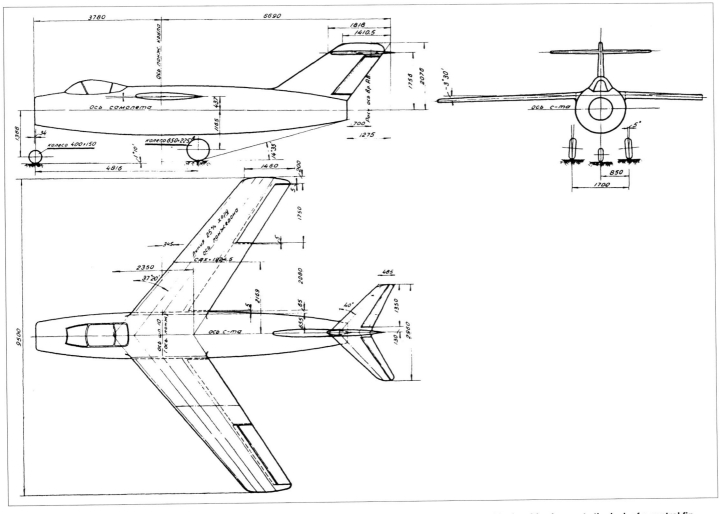

A provisional three-view drawing of the 'aircraft 168' fighter from the project documents. The wings are omitted in the side view; note the lack of a ventral fin.

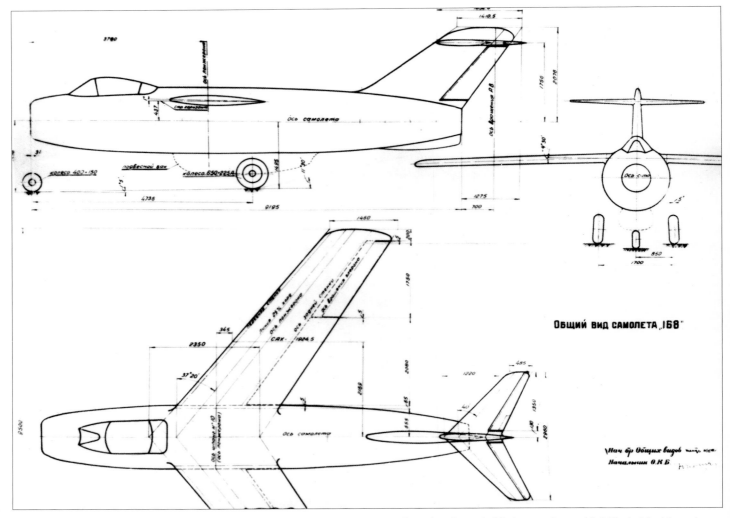

Above: Another drawing of the '168' from the project documents representing a later configuration; the ventral fin has now been added. The hatched lines show the conformal drop tank under the centre fuselage.

mainwheels forward; the aircraft had a rather narrow wheel track and a slight nose-up ground angle. The fuselage also accommodated four fuel tanks holding a total of 1,430 litres (314.6 Imp gal); provision was made for carrying a 610-litre (134.2 Imp gal) conformal drop tank under the fuselage on extended-range missions.

The '168' packed a mighty punch, the armament comprising one 37-mm (1.45 cal.) Nudelman N-37 cannon with an ammunition supply of 45 rounds and two 23-mm (.90 cal.) Nudelman/Rikhter NR-23 cannons with 100 rounds per gun. The cannons were buried in the forward fuselage underside, with the

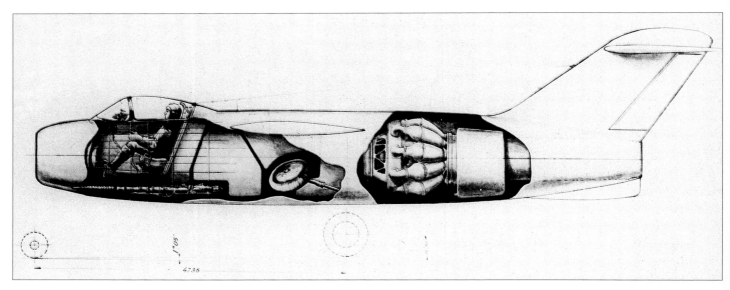

This cutaway drawing from the project documents shows the retracted position of the mainwheels stowing below the bladder tanks in the centre fuselage, the annular integral tank in the rear fuselage fitting around the engine jetpipe like a ring on a finger, and the cannons below the cockpit.

Above and below: The '168' was devoid of markings when it was rolled out. The nose-up ground angle and the narrow track of the landing gear are evident. Note the original short ventral fin and the landing/taxi light built into the air intake splitter.

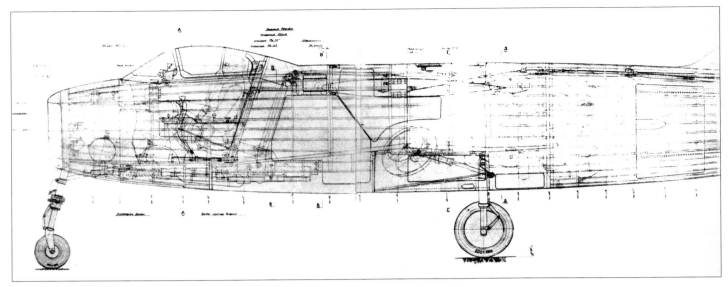

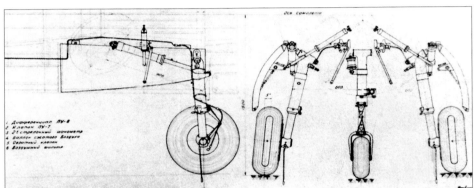

Above: A fragment of the manufacturing drawings issued for the '168', showing the internal structure of the fuselage (with a break point at frame 14), the complex shape of the bladder tanks and the placement of various equipment items.

Left: A drawing showing the landing gear design with skewed main gear fulcrum axles. Note that the mainwheel well doors have their own actuating rams rather than being mechanically linked to the oleo struts.

Below: Head-on view of the '168'; the wing anhedral is evident.

larger weapon to port and the two smaller ones to starboard.

According to MAP's prototype aircraft construction plan for 1948 'aircraft 168' was to have the following basic performance:

- top speed, 1,060 km/h (658 mph);
- climb time to 5,000 m (16,400 ft), 2.5 minutes;
- service ceiling, 14,000 m (45,930 ft);
- range at 10,000 m (32,810 ft), 1,200 km (745 miles);
- take-off run, 620 m (2,030 ft);
- landing run, 500 m (1,640 ft).

Prototype construction began in the summer of 1947 but completion was somewhat delayed by the late delivery of the aircraft's intended RR Nene engine (which was then entering production in the Soviet Union as the RD-45). Accordingly the manufacturer's flight tests had to be postponed until late April 1948. The maiden flight took place on 22nd April with OKB-301 chief test pilot Ivan Ye. Fyodorov at the controls. (22nd April just happens to be the birthday of Vladimir I. Lenin, the founder of the Soviet state.) In the course of the manufacturer's flight tests 'aircraft 168' was modified slightly in order to cure a tailplane vibration problem arising in certain flight modes and, for the first time in the OKB's practice, a hydraulic actuator was installed in the aileron control circuit.

On 18th July 1948 major air events took place in Leningrad, Kiev, Minsk and Odessa on occasion of Aviation Day. Moscow took a raincheck – bad weather forced the organisers to shift the Tushino event to the following weekend, 25th July. As was the case the year before, MAP was tasked with demonstrating the nation's latest achievements in fast jet aircraft technology for the world to see; therefore the air parade included a large number of combat jet prototypes. The formation was led by an RD-45 powered MiG-15, which streaked over Tushino at an altitude of 300-400 m (990-1,310 ft), doing 800 km/h (496 mph). It was followed, hot on its heels, by two Lavochkin fighter prototypes – the RD-500 powered '174' and the RD-45 powered '168', then the single-engined, single-seat Yak-25 fighter (the first aircraft to be thus designated), the Yak-23 and the twin-engined Alekseyev I-215 fighter (all powered by RD-500s and cruising at the same speed of 800 km/h). The Sukhoi OKB had also wanted to demonstrate its new Su-15 interceptor powered by two Nenes (the first aircraft to be thus designated), but the aircraft was not ready in time for the display. Next came several jet bomber prototypes in line-astern formation flying at 800 m (2,620 ft) and 650-680 km/h (403-422 mph), with the piston-engined – but nevertheless brand-new – Su-12 artillery spotter aircraft rounding up the show at 800-1,000 m (2,620-3,280 ft) and 350-390 km/h (217-242 mph).

Basic Specifications of 'Aircraft 168' as Recorded During Manufacturer's Flight Tests

Powerplant	1 x RD-45
Thrust, kgp (lbst)	2,270 (5,000)
Length overall	10.56 m (34 ft 7¾ in)
Wing span	9.5 m (31 ft 2⁴⁄₆₄ in)
Stabiliser span	3.0 m (9 ft 10⁷⁄₆₄ in)
Gross wing area, m² (sq ft)	18.08 (194.4)
Wing aspect ratio	5
Wing taper	1.61
Wing sweep at quarter-chord	37°20'
Wing anhedral	4°30'
Wing incidence	1°
Wing camber	0°30'
Mean aerodynamic chord (MAC)	1.9245 m (6 ft 3⁴⁸⁄₆₄ in)
Aileron area (total), m² (sq ft)	2.01 (21.61)
Aileron balance area (total), m² (sq ft)	0.747 (8.03)
Flap area (total), m² (sq ft)	2.75 (29.56)
Horizontal tail span	2.96 m (9 ft 8½ in)
Horizontal tail sweep at quarter-chord	40°
Horizontal tail aspect ratio	4.48
Horizontal tail taper	2.44
Horizontal tail incidence	+1° to –2° (set at 0° during tests)
Horizontal tail area, m² (sq ft)	2.55 (27.41)
Gross elevator area, m² (sq ft)	0.755 (8.11)
Elevator balance area (total), m² (sq ft)	0.151 (1.62)
Elevator trim tab area (total), m² (sq ft)	0.075 (0.806)
Vertical tail area, m² (sq ft)	3.38 (36.34)
Rudder area (overall), m² (sq ft)	0.718 (7.72)
Rudder balance area, m² (sq ft)	0.085 (0.91)
Landing gear track	1.7 m (5 ft 6¹⁵⁄₁₆ in)
Landing gear wheelbase	4.75 m (15 ft 7 in)
Empty weight, kg (lb)	3,111 (6,858)
Normal all-up weight, kg (lb)	4,580 (10,100)
Landing weight, kg (lb)	3,380 (7,450)
Useful load in normal AUW configuration, kg (lb):	
pilot (with parachute)	90 (198)
fuel	1,185 (2,610)
engine oil	5 (11)
armament	142 (313)
ammunition	173 (381)
CG position, % MAC:	
forward limit (normal AUW, gear retracted)	17.0
aft limit (landing approach with 10% fuel remaining, ammunition expended)	23.9
Maximum speed in level flight at 5,000 m (16,400 ft), km/h (mph)	1,080 (670)
Maximum Mach number attained	0.95
Landing speed, km/h (mph)	175 (108)
Climb time to 5,000 m, minutes	2.2
Service ceiling, m (ft)	14,500 (47,570)
Range on internal fuel, km (miles):	
at 1,000 m (3,280 ft)	750 (465)
at 5,000 m (16,400 ft)	1,020 (633)
at 10,000 m (32,810 ft)	1,500 (931)
Endurance in maximum range mode at 10,000 m	2 hrs 12 min
Take-off run (maximum TOW), m (ft)	500 (1,640)
Take-off distance to h=25 m (82 ft), m (ft)	1,050 (3,440)
Landing run (10% fuel remaining, ammunition expended), m (ft)	500 (1,640)
Landing distance from h=25 m (82 ft), m (ft)	1,130 (3,710) ‡
Armament	1 x 37-mm cannon
	2 x 23-mm cannons

Speed Performance of 'Aircraft 168' in Level Flight as Recorded During Manufacturer's Flight Tests (engine speed 12,300 rpm)

Altitude, m (ft)	Maximum speed, km/h (mph)	Mach number
3,000 (9,840)	1,072 (665)	0.900
4,000 (13,120)	1,078 (669)	0.920
5,000 (16,400)	1,080 (670)	0.934
6,000 (19,685)	1,076 (668)	0.942
7,000 (22,965)	1,066 (662)	0.946
8,000 (26,250)	1,056 (656)	0.950

Climb Times and Vertical Speeds of 'Aircraft 168'

Altitude, m (ft)	Indicated airspeed, km/h (mph)	Rate of climb, m/sec (ft/min)	Climb time, minutes
0 (sea level)	640 (397)	46.4 (7.930)	–
1,000 (3,280)	620 (385)	44.3 (7,570)	0,45
2,000 (6,560)	600 (372)	42.4 (7,250)	0,85
3,000 (9,840)	575 (357)	40.0 (6,840)	1,30
4,000 (13,120)	550 (341)	37.3 (6,380)	1,70
5,000 (16,400)	525 (326)	34.6 (5,910)	2,16
6,000 (19,685)	520 (323)	32.0 (5,470)	2,60
7,000 (22,965)	475 (295)	28.8 (4,920)	3,20
8,000 (26,250)	450 (279)	25.6 (4,380)	3,85
9,000 (29,530)	420 (260)	22.4 (3,830)	4,60
10,000 (32,810)	390 (242)	19.0 (3,250)	5,60

Notes:
1. The take-off weight during these tests was 4,460 kg (9,830 lb).
2. The service ceiling of 14,500 m (47,570 ft) was obtained by extrapolating the aircraft's vertical speed/altitude ratio.
3. Calculations for an AUW of 4,580 kg (10,100 lb) give a time of 2.2 minutes required to reach 5,000 m.

The manufacturer's flight tests of the '168' were successfully completed on 24th August 1948 after 42 flights. They included bore-sighting the cannons on the ground and air-to-air gunnery sorties. It was clear from the test results that OKB-301 had succeeded in creating a capable fighter. The results of the manufacturer's flight tests are given in the following tables.

The '168' was stable and handled well in all flight modes, performing aerobatics with ease. The airframe and landing gear design made it possible to operate from semi-prepared dirt or grass runways as well as from paved ones. The concluding part of the manufacturer's flight test report stated that *'the government's basic performance target has been met in full. The results obtained in the course of the manufacturer's flight tests exceed the figures stipulated by the government directive.'*

Upon completion of the tests the '168' was transferred to GK NII VVS for state acceptance trials. These began at Novofyodorovka AB in Saki on the Crimea Peninsula, the Ukraine, in October 1948 with Col. V. I. Khomyakov as project test pilot. The trials showed that the aircraft outperformed all of the other new Soviet jet fighters undergoing tests at the time. With an empty weight of 2,973 kg (6,554 lb) and an all-up weight of 4,412 kg (9,726 lb), the '168' attained a maximum speed of 1,084 km/h (673 mph) at 2,750 m (9,020 ft), which equalled Mach 0.982. The fighter climbed to 5,000 m (16,400 ft) in two minutes flat; the service ceiling was 14,570 m (47,800 ft) and range with a full fuel load was 1,275 km (791 miles). Praising the fighter's handling, the military test pilots pointed out nevertheless that the vertical tail area was insufficient. This defect was cured by fitting a larger ventral fin.

The state acceptance trials of the '168' were marred by an incident – the canopy glazing shattered when Khomyakov fired all three cannons in a salvo at 15,000 m (49,210 ft). Passing out as the cockpit decompressed, the pilot involuntarily put the machine into a dive; luckily he regained consciousness at 4,000 m (13,120 ft) and succeeded in making a recovery when the aircraft had accelerated almost to Mach 1.

The state acceptance trials were completed on 19th February 1949 and the fighter was recommended for production and service. By then, however, the MiG-15 and the La-15 (La-174; see next chapter) were already in production, having completed their state acceptance trials with good results ahead of the '168'. Therefore there was no point in launching production; it was a case of being in the right place at the wrong time. Later, the '168' prototype was refitted with a more powerful Klimov VK-1 turbojet – an uprated version of the RD-45F delivering 2,700 kgp (5,950 lbst) for take-off, but after only three flights in this configuration the government issued orders to terminate the programme.

It should be noted that this was by no means a unanimous decision; many high-ranking government and Air Force officials were opposed to the closure of the programme. Thus, on 2nd July 1949 the Communist Party branch at GK NII VVS had a meeting, writing an official letter to Council of Ministers Chairman Vyacheslav M. Molotov. The institute thereby requested permission to perform manufacturer's flight tests and subsequently state acceptance trials of the '168' fighter refitted with the VK-1 engine and (at a later date) with new wings swept back 45° at quarter-chord, asserting that this aircraft would have more refined aerodynamics and higher performance than the MiG-15. Still, the decision in favour of the latter aircraft had been taken at the top level and there was no changing it. The later MiG-15*bis* powered by the VK-1 engine could barely come close to the performance demonstrated by the '168' with the smaller engine, and even that was almost a year later (in late 1949/early 1950).

Basic Specifications of 'Aircraft 168' as Recorded During State Acceptance Trials

Powerplant	1 x RD-45
Thrust, kgp (lbst)	2,270 (5,000)
Empty weight, kg (lb)	2,973 (6,554)
All-up weight, kg (lb)	4,412 (9,726)
Fuel capacity, litres (Imp gal):	
internal	1,230 (270.6)
drop tank	610 (134.2)
Maximum speed at 2,750 m (9,020 ft)	1,084 (673)
Climb time to 5,000 m, minutes	2.0
Service ceiling, m (ft)	14,570 (47,800)
Range on internal fuel, km (miles)	1,275 (791)
Endurance in maximum range mode at 10,000 m	2 hrs 12 min

Chapter 3

The Production Jet

'Aircraft 174' (La-15) Tactical Fighter Prototype

As noted in the introduction, the purchase of the Rolls-Royce Nene I/II and Rolls-Royce Derwent V turbojet engines shortly after the war gave a powerful impetus to the Soviet aircraft industry, influencing both airframe and engine development. Once the British engines had been mastered in production by Soviet plants as the RD-45 and the RD-500 respectively, Soviet aircraft design bureaux were in a position to develop new-generation combat aircraft. In particular, a Council of Ministers directive dated 11th March 1947 tasked several Soviet 'fighter makers' with creating new jet fighters. This document required the fighters to have a maximum speed of 1,000-1,020 km/h (621-633 mph) and a service ceiling of 13,000 m (42,650 ft); range at 10,000 m (32,810 ft) was to be 1,200 km (745 miles) on internal fuel only, increasing to 1,600 km (993 miles) with drop tanks. In keeping with the Air Force's requirements the armament was to comprise at least three cannons of 23-mm or

heavier calibre. Since the fighters were supposed to operate at altitudes in excess of 10,000 m, they had to feature pressurised cockpits and airbrakes. The directive set a very tough deadline – the new fighters were to be ready for state acceptance trials by December 1947 at the latest.

The Yakovlev OKB was the first past the post, offering the Yak-23 light fighter powered by the Derwent V (RD-500). Although this machine did not meet the specified performance target and armament requirements, at least it was more advanced than the Soviet Air Force's then-current jet fighters; thus it was accepted for production and service until something better came along. Yet the Air Force and MAP demanded higher performance, urging the Mikoyan and Lavochkin OKBs to develop swept-wing fighters. Both bureaux had been designing their new fighters around the more powerful Nene II (RD-45F) from the outset. Mikoyan brought

Above: Delays with the RD-45 forced Semyon A. Lavochkin to develop the '174' – a scaled-down '168'.

out the I-310 – the prototype of the world-famous MiG-15; Lavochkin's competing 'aircraft 168' has been described in the previous chapter. However, these programmes were facing delays because of the temporary unavailability of the RD-45 engine whose production in the Soviet Union was only just

The first prototype of the scaled-down fighter – the '174' – at Zhukovskiy in December 1948. The original short ventral fin, the smooth main gear doors and the original canopy design (with a semi-elliptical bulletproof windshield and transverse frame members) are clearly visible, as is the single NR-23 cannon to port.

Above and below: Two more aspects of the '174', showing the muzzle openings and spent case ejector ports of the two starboard NR-23 cannons. The fuselage break point at frame 14 is clearly visible. Again, the fighter is devoid of all markings.

The S-1 – the first prototype of the rival Mikoyan I-310 (later redesignated MiG-15) was tested concurrently. The difference in the two fighters' design is striking; the I-310 had mid-set wings and a tail unit with a more pronounced cruciform layout. Note the exposed cannon barrels.

beginning. Conversely, the Derwent V had been in production in Great Britain for quite a while by then, and deliveries of these turbo-jets to the Soviet Union had begun as early as mid-1947.

Here it is worth mentioning that OKB-155's Chief Designer Artyom I. Mikoyan was in an advantageous position; his brother Anastas I. Mikoyan was a key figure in the Soviet government at the time, which meant the Mikoyan OKB could count on priority deliveries of Nene II engines for its aircraft. Semyon A. Lavochkin did not have such influential friends and relatives in high places, and obtaining the Nene became a problem. Hence, as an insurance policy, he decided to design a scaled-down version of the '168' powered by the Derwent V but having the same design performance. In September 1947 Lavochkin wrote an official letter to Minister of Aircraft Industry Aleksey I. Shakhoorin, requesting permission to build such an aircraft instead of the '168'. The minister gave the go-ahead but stated that the fighter would have experimental status and was to be developed in addition to the '168', not instead of it; the assignment to build the latter aircraft was still there. As Russian folk wisdom goes, 'initiative is punishable'.

The scaled-down version received the in-house designation 'aircraft 174'. With very lit-

tle time at their disposal, the designers tried to make maximum use of the design features incorporated in the '168' in order to make the year-end deadline. The aircraft shared the larger fighter's layout with shoulder-mounted swept wings, cruciform swept tail surfaces and circular-section fuselage – logically enough, since the smaller Derwent engine chosen for it was also similar in design to the Nene powering the '168'. Moreover, structural components and equipment items from the '168' were used insofar as possible.

As in the case of the '168', the wings of the '174' were swept back 37°20' at quarter-chord. As for the cruciform tail surfaces, this arrangement had become standard for Soviet jet fighters developed in the late 1940s and early 1950s (with a few exceptions). The main landing gear units retracted forward into the fuselage, leaving the wings aerodynamically 'clean' and uncompromised by wheel wells, thus increasing their structural stiffness. In keeping with the Air Force's requirements the rear fuselage incorporated hydraulically actuated airbrakes; the cockpit was pressurised, which was also a requirement of the military. The armament consisted of three 23-mm (.90 cal.) Nudelman/Rikhter NR-23 cannons with 100 rpg. These were aimed by means of an ASP-1N computing gunsight (*avtomatich-eskiy strelkovyy pritsel*) – a Soviet-built copy

of the British Mk IID gunsight. The sight had a gyro and a movable grid; it generated the appropriate target lead angles with regard to the flight level, ambient temperature and the fighter's angle speed (pitch/yaw/roll rates). The ASP-1N was a bulky item; yet this short-coming was outweighed by the fact that it ensured accurate gunnery at up to 800 m (2,625 ft) range versus the predecessors' 400 m (1,310 ft).

Development of the '174' proceeded at an incredible pace, and the design stage was completed in December 1947. At that time the Mikoyan OKB was close to completing the design work on the I-310 (*izdeliye* S) powered by the Nene. However, even with Mikoyan's heavy connections, the intended 2,270-kgp (5,000-lbst) version was still unavailable by the time the first prototype (designated S-1) was completed. Alarmed by this, Mikoyan ordered that the lower-powered Nene I delivering 2,040 kgp (4,500 lbst) be installed in the S-01 so that flight tests could begin. The second prototype (S-02) had the uprated RD-45F engine from the outset.

The prototypes of the Lavochkin and Mikoyan fighters were completed almost concurrently; the I-310 (S-1) was delivered to the Mikoyan OKB's flight test facility at the LII airfield in Zhukovskiy on 24th December 1947, while the '174' arrived at the co-located

Lavochkin OKB test facility a week later, on New Year's Eve. The maiden flights followed almost immediately – again with roughly a week's interval; the I-310 took to the air on 30th December, while the '174' first flew on 8th January 1948. Thus began the manufacturer's flight tests of the competing fighters.

OKB-301's chief test pilot Ivan Ye. Fyodorov (HSU) was assigned project test pilot for the '174'. The very first test flights revealed a defect that turned into a major headache for the designers: certain flight modes were accompanied by severe vibration in the pitch control channel. The problem persisted throughout the manufacturer's flight tests. Many possible causes were considered and various ways of tackling the problem were tried without success; these included revisions to the elevator hinge brackets, the landing gear door hinges, the engine mount, the fuel system and so on. It took a lot of flights with a set of test equipment recording various flight parameters to establish the true cause: it turned out that the structural frequencies of the stabilisers and the fuselage coincided. The OKB quickly designed and fitted a stiffer horizontal tail; that took care of the problem – the vibrations were almost gone. After that the first stage of the manufacturer's flight tests was quickly concluded in April 1948.

Other problems cropping up at this stage included excessively high stick forces in the aileron control circuit and excessively high rudder pedal forces. It was obvious that the fighter needed powered controls; therefore the engineers decided to install a hydraulic actuator in the aileron control circuit of the '168' and '174' fighters.

Unfortunately the first prototype 'aircraft 174' crashed before the manufacturer's flight tests could be completed. In the afternoon of 11th May 1948 Ivan Ye. Fyodorov was making his third flight in the '174' that day – the final flight under the aircraft's test programme. The test mission was to assess the fighter's stability and handling at 4,000 m (13,120 ft) and 8,000 m (26,250 ft). As the aircraft accelerated to 680-690 km/h (422-428 mph) at 8,000 m, severe vibration set in again, intensifying rapidly. The preventive measures used successfully hitherto proved of no avail; worse, the elevator control circuit failed, rendering the aircraft uncontrollable and leaving the pilot no choice but to abandon ship. To top it all, the cartridge-fired ejection seat was use-

Above left: The second prototype, 'aircraft 174D', which replaced the crashed first prototype in the test programme. It is seen from the roof of a hangar to show the wing and horizontal tail planform.

Left: The '174D' differed outwardly in having a revised canopy having a rectangular windshield and a rear portion minus transverse frame.

less because, ironically, the powder cartridge had to meet, coupled with both design teams' had been removed at the pilot's request – Fyodorov had feared that the seat might fire spontaneously because of the vibration. The only option was to bail out the old-fashioned way; with immense difficulty Fyodorov managed to do it, parachuting to safety.

'Aircraft 174D' Tactical Fighter Prototype

The manufacturer's flight tests were completed, using the second prototype, which bore the in-house designation 'aircraft 174D'; the D suffix stood for *dooblyor* (lit. 'understudy'), the Soviet term for second prototypes used until the late 1960s. Construction of this aircraft, which proceeded in parallel with the first prototype's flight tests, was stepped up while the '174' was undergoing modifications. The '174D' was completed on 10th June 1948, making its first flight just two days later with Ivan Ye. Fyodorov at the controls; it incorporated all the revisions made on the first prototype by then. This aircraft was earmarked for the type's state acceptance trials.

Early test flights in the '174D' showed that the vibration problem had been cured completely and the controls were lighter. After making a mere seven flights under the manufacturer's flight test programme, which was then declared completed, the '174D' was submitted for state acceptance trials on 22nd June 1948 – a month later than the S-1 and S-2 prototypes of the competing I-310 (the latter had by then been redesignated MiG-15).

Actually, however, the state acceptance trials did not begin until 1st August 1948, and the aircraft lacked the conformal drop tank intended for it. There were two reasons for this delay – firstly, the aircraft was being prepared for the traditional Aviation Day flypast at Moscow-Tushino; secondly, the military had voiced a few complaints concerning the aircraft, which had to be dealt with before it could be accepted for trials. Andrey G. Kochetkov was the GK NII VVS project test pilot for the '174D', with engineer Chernyavskiy in charge of the trials. Test pilots Pyotr M. Stefanovskiy, A. G. Proshakov, V. I. Khomyakov, Ivan M. Dzyuba, A. G. Terent'yev, V. P. Trofimov and Leonid M. Koovshinov also flew the fighter at GK NII VVS.

Thus the two contenders for the Soviet Air Force's new tactical fighter type – the MiG-15 and Lavochkin's 'aircraft 174D' – were undergoing state acceptance trials at the same time. In effect, this was a fly-off, though the term was unknown in the Soviet Union.

The novel features embodied in these aircraft gave the Mikoyan and Lavochkin fighters very high performance by the day's standards – and broadly comparable performance at that. On the other hand, the tight development schedules which both OKBs

had to meet, coupled with both design teams' desire to get ahead of the competitor, inevitably led to design faults and flaws, of which both fighters had quite a few. The speed envelope was almost identical – the MiG-15 had a top speed of 1,042 km/h (647 mph) at 2,620 m (8,600 ft) while the '174D' attained 1,040 km/h (646 mph) at 3,000 m (9,840 ft). By virtue of its higher thrust/weight ratio the MiG-15 had a better rate of climb, attaining 5,000 m (16,400 ft) in 2.3 minutes versus three minutes flat for the Lavochkin fighter. On the other hand, the latter showed better turning, acceleration and deceleration characteristics; the better deceleration was due to the fact that the S-1 and S-2 lacked the envisaged airbrakes, whereas the '174D' had them. The Lavochkin fighter showed marginally better field performance but the effect was spoiled by the frequent mainwheel tyre failures, which were caused by the high loads the wheels were subjected to. Both fighters exceeded their stipulated range of 1,200 km (745 miles) on internal fuel – at 10,000 m (32,810 ft) the MiG-15 and the '174D' had a maximum range of 1,395 km (866 miles) and 1,300 km (807 miles).

Thanks to its cleanly designed airframe the '174D' also exhibited better stability and handling than the MiG-15, especially at high speeds. The MiG-15 suffered from poor aileron efficiency and high stick forces in the aileron control circuit – the prototypes did not yet have powered ailerons. Later the MiG was found to be suffering from other design flaws, including a tendency to drop a wing, called *val'ozhka* in Russian, which had first manifested itself on the third prototype. At high speed the aircraft would start rolling; the stick force required to counter this motion grew quickly as speed increased, and the pilot was physically unable to keep the wings level. The roots of the problem lay in the insufficient torsional stiffness of the MiG-15's wings, which were weakened by the mainwheel wells, and insufficient aileron authority.

The '174D' also had certain deficiencies which the military pointed out at an early stage of the state acceptance trials. These included excessive lateral stability coupled with insufficient directional stability and excessively high stick forces in the aileron control circuit. OKB-301 engineers were aware of this back at the manufacturer's test stage and sought measures to improve the situation. In the course of the state acceptance trials the fighter's wing anhedral was increased from 4° to 5°20' and a new ventral fin was fitted to improve directional stability. The most important change, however, concerned the control system, which now featured a hydraulic actuator in the aileron control circuit. These modifications improved the fighter's handling appreciably.

Above and below: The '174D' at GK NII VVS during Stage A of the state acceptance trials; note the distinctive hexagonal concrete slabs of the hardstand at Chkalovskaya AB. The aircraft has been modified by fitting a larger ventral fin; note also the large gun blast plate on the underside of the nose.

Above and below: Two more views of the '174D' at Chkalovskaya AB; the diminutive fighter sat high above the ground on its tall undercarriage, an impression enhanced by the narrow wheel track. Note the Tupolev Tu-2 bomber (apparently a testbed of some kind) in the background.

Top and above: The '174D' is seen here in its ultimate form at plant No.301, showing the bulged canopy with a new semi-elliptical windshield and the addition of an aerial mast aft of the cockpit. This was, in effect, the production configuration submitted for checkout trials in December 1949.

In a shallow dive the '174D' reached a maximum speed of Mach 0.93 (the never-exceed speed stipulated by Chief Designer Semyon A. Lavochkin for this aircraft) at 8,200 m (26,900 ft); the aircraft handled normally at this speed, showing no tendency to go out of control. The state acceptance trials report noted that *'…good longitudinal stability at high Mach numbers is this aircraft's main merit. All aircraft tested previously became statically unstable in the longitudinal control channel at lower Mach numbers'*.

Yet the MiG-15 prototypes were not the military test pilots' only benchmark for assessing the new Lavochkin fighter. The same trials report also pointed out that in some respects the '174D' was inferior to the

identically powered Yak-25 single-seat tactical fighter (the first aircraft to bear this designation) that had passed its state acceptance trials earlier. In particular, the '174D' was 50 km/h (31 mph) slower at sea level, albeit 68 km/h (42 mph) faster than the Yak at 3,000 m (9,840 ft). The straight-wing Yak-25 had 71 km (44 miles) shorter range but displayed better turning times, a better rate of climb, a higher service ceiling and better field performance. Thus, despite all their advantages, swept wings could be a liability sometimes; the Yak-25's better field performance was due exactly to the unswept wings giving a lower approach speed. The test pilots agreed that the '174D' presented no problems for the average-skilled pilot but was rather demand-

ing during manoeuvres in a climb; its acceleration parameters were superior to those of the MiG-15 but inferior to those of the Yak-25.

The state acceptance trials report further said that *'…if the air-to-air engagement begins at indicated airspeeds of 750 km/h [465 mph] and higher (that is, with a closing rate in excess of 1,500 km/h [931 mph]), the pilots quickly lose sight of each other due to the wide trajectories of the manoeuvres and the excessively high G loads of long duration experienced during these manoeuvres'*. The trials included a mock dogfight between the '174D' and the piston-engined La-9; the jet fighter came out on top, but the report stated nevertheless that it was inadvisable to engage in a dogfight with the piston-engined machine

Above and below: The same aircraft at GK NII VVS in the course of the State checkout trials. The '174D' was still unmarked at this stage.

Above: The military test pilots who took part in the state acceptance trials of the '174D'. Left to right: Pyotr M. Stefanovskiy, Ivan M. Dzyuba, Leonid M. Koovshinov and A. G. Terent'yev. Note the different uniforms – Stefanovskiy is depicted wearing the older-style uniform.

Below: Andrey G. Kochetkov, the fighter's project test pilot at GK NII VVS.

Specifications of the '174' and '174D' as Recorded During Manufacturer's Flight Tests and State Acceptance Trials

	'174'	'174D'	
	Manufacturer's flight tests	Manufacturer's flight tests	State acceptance trials
Powerplant	RR Derwent V	RR Derwent V	
Thrust, kgp (lbst)	1,590 (3,500)	1,590 (3,500)	
Length overall	n.a.	9.56 m (31 ft 4⅝ in)	
Height on ground	n.a.	3.8 m (12 ft 5³⁹⁄₆₄ in)	
Wing span	n.a.	8.83 m (28 ft 11⅝ in)	
Wing area, m² (sq ft)	16.16 (173.76)	16.16 (173.76)	
Empty weight, kg (lb)	n.a.	n.a.	2,433 (5,363)
All-up weight, kg (lb)	3,600 (7,940) or 3,660 (8,070)	n.a.	3,708 (8,174)
Fuel capacity, litres (Imp gal)	n.a.	1,110 (244.2)	1,110 (244.2)
Maximum speed, km/h (mph)	1,038 (644)	n.a.	1,040 (646)
at altitude	4,000 (13,120)		3,000 (9,840)
Maximum speed at 8,000 m (26,250 ft), km/h (mph)	1,004 (623)	1,024 (636)	1,020 (633)
Climb time, minutes:			
to 5,000 m (16,400 ft)	2.8	2.95	3.0
to 10,000 m (32,810 ft)	7.0	n.a.	9.2
Rate of climb at sea level, m/sec (ft/min)	n.a.	n.a.	33.0 (6,490)
Service ceiling, m (ft)	n.a.	14,200 (46,590)	14,600 (47,900)
Range at 10,000 m, km (miles)	1,220 (757)	n.a.	1,300 (807)
Maximum endurance on internal fuel at 10,000 m	1 hr 56 min	n.a.	2 hrs 28 min
360° turn time at 5,000 m, sec	n.a.	n.a.	37.5
Altitude gain in a combat turn at 5,000 m, m (ft)	n.a.	n.a.	2,350 (7,710)
Take-off run, m (ft) *	590 (1,935)	n.a.	595 (1,950)
Take-off distance, m (ft) *	n.a.	n.a.	1,370 (4,490)
Landing run, m (ft) *	400 (1,310)	n.a.	550 (1,800)
Landing distance, m (ft) *	n.a.	n.a.	1,050 (3,440)
Armament	3 x 23-mm cannons 300 rounds	n.a.	3 x 23-mm cannons 300 rounds

* The field performance was measured on a concrete runway; airbrakes were used to shorten the landing run.

in the horizontal plane. Live weapons trials at various altitudes up to 13,000 m (42,650 ft) gave good results, confirming that the '174D' was fit for service.

The state acceptance trials of the new Lavochkin fighter were completed on 25th September 1948. The State commissions supervising the trials of the MiG-15 and the '174D' noted that the performance of both fighters was generally high and, despite the deficiencies discovered in the course of the trials, both types were recommended for production and service. A while earlier, on 23rd August 1948, the Council of Ministers had issued directive No.3210-1303 ordering the MiG-15 and the La-174 (this was the provisional service designation of the '174D') into production; the MiG-15 had completed its state acceptance trials by then. The La-174 was to be manufactured by two plants – No.21 in Gor'kiy, central Russia (the main

Performance of the '174D' in Vertical Manoeuvres as Recorded During State Acceptance Trials

Manoeuvre	Altitude at entry, m (ft)	Altitude at exit, m (ft)	Altitude change, m (ft)	Entry speed, km/h (mph)	Exit speed, km/h (mph)	Speed change, km/h (mph)	Time, sec
Combat turn	2,240 (6,690)	4,860 (15,940)	2,620 (8,590)	820 (509)	310 (192)	510 (316)	35
ditto	5,150 (16,900)	7,500 (24,600)	2,350 (7,710)	740 (459)	310 (192)	430 (267)	42
ditto	8,030 (26,345)	10,150 (33,300)	2,120 (6,955)	634 (393)	320 (198)	314 (195)	45
Split-S	8,320 (27,300)	6,370 (20,900)	1,950 (6,400)	280 (174)	620 (385)	340 (211)	34
Loop	5,000 (16,400)	5,260 (17,260)	260 (850)	740 (459)	634 (393)	106 (65)	46
Immelmann turn	5,070 (16,630)	7,160 (23,490)	2,090 (6,860)	760 (472)	348 (216)	412 (255)	27

Diving Characteristics of the '174D' as Recorded During State Acceptance Trials

Dive angle	Entry altitude, m (ft)	Pullout altitude, m (ft)	Altitude loss, m (ft)	Entry speed, km/h (mph)	Pullout km/h (mph)	Speed gain, km/h (mph)	G load during pullout
20°	5,840 (19,160) /	2,000 (6,560) /	3,840 (12,600) /	306 (190) /	830 (515) /	524 (325) /	3.3 /
	5,800 (19,030)	2,400 (7,870)	3,400 (11,150)	312 (193)	675 (419)	363 (225)	2.3
30°	5,860 (19,225) /	2,500 (8,200) /	3,360 (11,020) /	300 (186) /	840 (521) /	540 (335) /	3.9 /
	5,770 (18,930)	2,350 (7,710)	3,420 (11,220)	328 (203)	744 (462)	416 (258)	2.9
40°	5,800 (19,030) /	2,680 (8,790) /	3,120 (10,240) /	318 (197) /	840 (521) /	522 (324) /	4.4 /
	5,780 (18,960)	2,100 (6,890)	3,680 (12,070)	318 (197)	785 (487)	467 (290)	3.5
50°	5,800 (19,030) /	2,460 (8,070) /	3,340 (10,960) /	302 (187) /	885 (549) /	583 (362) /	5.0 /
	5,820 (19,090)	2,190 (7,185)	3,630 (11,910)	324 (201)	805 (500)	481 (298)	3.9

Note: The first series of figures for each dive angle refers to the results obtained without using airbrakes; the second series is the results obtained with airbrakes deployed.

manufacturer), and No.292 in Saratov, southern Russia. The directive required the Mikoyan and Lavochkin OKBs to rectify all the faults detected in the course of the trials and submit the modified fighters to GK NII VVS for checkout trials in November 1948; full-scale production of both types was to commence in January 1949.

The following table gives the performance of the '174' and '174D' prototypes.

Checkout trials of the '174D' fighter modified in accordance with the State commission's recommendations began on 8th December 1948. Among other things, the aircraft was fitted with a new bulged cockpit canopy offering better lateral and downward visibility. A mast for the communications radio's wire aerial was installed aft of the cockpit in order to increase communications range to the specified 120 km (74.5 miles). The fuel system now featured a device ensuring uninterrupted fuel feed to the engine under negative-G conditions. These and other minor modifications improved the aircraft's operation, but they had a price: because of the extra weight the top speed was reduced somewhat, being 1,026 km/h (637 mph) at 3,000 m (9,840 ft).

Some of the faults were not addressed at this stage; the worst of these was the mainwheels which were poorly suited to the aircraft's operational parameters. The wheels were subjected to excessive loads that peaked at 1,550 kg (3,420 lb) when the aircraft was parked, which was way beyond their design limit of 1,250 kg (2,755 lb). This caused the wheels to overheat when the brakes were applied; it also caused the wheel bearings and tyres to disintegrate and increased the wear and tear on the brakes and tyres. (Later, production La-15s were fitted with larger mainwheels and the mainwheel well doors were bulged slightly to accommodate them; this resolved the problem.) Still, this glitch did not affect the generally positive assessment of the fighter; the modified '174D' was chosen as the pattern aircraft for series production.

La-15 (La-174, *Izdeliye* 52) Production Tactical Fighter

At the end of 1948 preparations for series production of the MiG-15 and the La-174 were going full steam ahead at the two abovemen-

Above: A series of photos from the La-15's structural design manual. Typically of Soviet official documents of the day, the photos are so heavily retouched that they look like pencil drawings.

tioned production plants – No.21 in Gor'kiy and No.292 in Saratov. The former factory, which was selected as the main manufacturer of the La-174, had started gearing up to build the type as early as 15th September when it took delivery of a set of manufacturing drawings from OKB-301. However, the drawings were for the '174D' prototype whose airframe

A still from a cine film showing 196th IAP La-15s on the flight line at Kubinka AB during service tests, with '201 White' (c/n 52210201) nearest. The red nose colours were applied for the 1949 Aviation Day parade.

structure was ill suited for mass production; many parts required machining and trimming to make them fit, which was no problem for the OKB's experimental plant but was bound to cause problems in mass production. According to the production plan for 1949 the Gor'kiy plant alone was to turn out 650 La-174s; such a large production scale

required an airframe that was easier to build and better suited to production technologies. Hence the design office of plant No.21 had to redesign many of the fighter's structural elements (with the Chief Designer's approval) within the shortest possible time and develop the appropriate jigs and tooling anew.

The Gor'kiy aircraft factory had its own system of in-house product codes, and the La-174 was assigned the internal designation *izdeliye* 52. The first Gor'kiy-built example (construction number 52210101 – that is, *izdeliye* 52, plant No.21, Batch 01, 01st aircraft in the batch) was completed in late December 1948; the second and third machines followed in January 1949. Quite apart from the extremely tight production schedule, production was severely complicated by the seemingly endless stream of design changes and amendments handed down from the OKB. In the first quarter of 1949 alone, plant No.21 introduced more than 3,000 changes and refinements on the La-174 production line and redesigned 85 of the fighter's structural elements, which reduced the overall time required to build the aircraft by 1,200 man-hours.

Despite the inevitable difficulties associated with the learning curve, the plant steadily built up production of the new fighter, turning out five La-174s in February 1949, 13 in March and 21 in April. Also in April 1949, plant No.292

Above: Gor'kiy-built La-15 '202 White' (c/n 52210202) was used in a special spinning tests programme by GK NII VVS during the checkout trials. Here it is seen with the special spin recovery rockets under the wings.
Below: The same aircraft with what appears to be a cine camera pointing at the tail surfaces installed on the starboard wingtip. In flight, the La-15 had a graceful arrow-like appearance.

Above: Three red-nosed La-15s at Kubinka AB, which also had hexagonal concrete slabs on the hardstands. Different production batches had serials of different colours, as illustrated by '201 White' and '371 Blue' (c/n 52210317); the nearest aircraft also has a blue serial (possibly '318 Blue').

rolled out its first La-174. The first batch of 20 fighters accepted by the military inspectors in March was promptly delivered to the 196th IAP (*istrebitel'nyy aviapolk* – fighter regiment) at Kubinka airbase west of Moscow; this unit was to evaluate the new type.

Unfortunately a tragic event that occurred on 3rd February 1949 – the fatal crash of the closely related 'aircraft 176' experimental fighter (see Chapter 5) – was to have, albeit indirectly, a negative effect on the La-174's ultimate fate. Even though the crash had clearly been caused by pilot error, and regardless even of the fact that the '176' was the first Soviet aircraft to exceed Mach 1 (no small achievement), some people in the MAP top brass and the Soviet government were now regarding the Lavochkin OKB in general and the La-174 in particular with a jaundiced eye.

Nevertheless, work on the MiG-15 and La-174 programmes alike was stepped up dramatically in April 1949. Moreover, it was then that the La-174 received its ultimate service designation, La-15, after the Council of Ministers had endorsed the fighter's state acceptance trials and checkout trials reports. OKB-301 was instructed to incorporate the modifications recommended by GK NII VVS on one of the production La-15s and to build two prototypes of a two-seat trainer version. Furthermore, Chief Designer Vladimir Ya. Klimov, who had led the effort to copy the Rolls-Royce Derwent V and put it into production as the RD-500, was tasked with developing an afterburning version of this engine jointly with TsIAM for the purpose of improving the La-15's performance. This work was begun in response to a Lavochkin OKB request.

Yet, barely three weeks later the La-15's fortunes suffered a dramatic downturn. The event that precipitated this was the successful completion of the VK-1 turbojet's state acceptance trials. The VK-1, an uprated Soviet version of the RD-45 (RR Nene) delivering 2,700 kgp (5,950 lbst), opened the possibilities for further enhancing the flight performance of combat aircraft; thus the less powerful RD-500 immediately lost its appeal. Hence the Council of Ministers drafted a new directive requiring jet combat aircraft production to be reorganised; apart from a specialised interceptor for the IA PVO, only one jet fighter and only one jet tactical bomber were to remain in production – both of them powered by VK-1 engines. It was decided to terminate La-15 production in Gor'kiy; instead, plant No.21 was to start preparing for MiG-15 production. No decision concerning

An interesting still from a cine film showing the same La-15 '317 Blue' in natural metal colours taking off in formation with a red-nosed La-15 '112 White' (c/n 52210112); apparently the red paint was removed from this aircraft after the parade.

plant No.292 was taken just yet, but it was obvious that La-15 production in Saratov would not last long either.

In fairness, it should be pointed out that the MiG-15, which was built on a much larger scale, was somewhat inferior in performance to the Lavochkin 'aircraft 168' experimental fighter powered by the same engine, to say nothing of the '176'. On the other hand, it was much better suited for mass production and easier to build. A disconcerted Semyon A. Lavochkin wrote personally to Iosif V. Stalin, questioning the choice of the MiG-15 as the fighter selected for production. However, the Soviet leader did not favour aircraft whose reputation had been marred by accidents. Being aware of this, Lavochkin mentioned only the '168' in his letter because this aircraft, which had successfully passed its state acceptance trials, had considerable commonality with the La-15 and would be a better choice to replace the latter aircraft on the Gor'kiy production line. He chose not to mention the '176' because this aircraft had crashed, which would overshadow its supersonic performance in Stalin's view.

Still, the Soviet government stuck unflinchingly to its decision. The decision to produce only the MiG-15 instead of two fighter types was formally approved on 14th May 1949 with the consent of the Air Force (after all, the MiG-15 met nearly all of the Air Force's requirements).

Meanwhile, on 19th May 1949 the 196th IAP commenced service trials of the 20 La-15s it had received; these were Gor'kiy-built examples from production batches 1 and 2. One more Gor'kiy-built La-15, serialled '202 White' (c/n 52210202), was turned over to GK NII VVS for the purpose of holding State checkout trials.

The fighter had an empty weight of 2,575 kg (5,680 lb) and a take-off weight of 3,830-3,850 kg (8,440-8,490 lb). The basic performance differed little from that of the '174D' prototype, which, as the reader remembers, had been designated as the pattern aircraft for series production. The production La-15 had a top speed of 1,026 km/h (637 mph) at 3,000 m (9,840 ft) and reached an altitude of 5,000 m (16,400 ft) in 3.1 minutes. The service ceiling and range had deteriorated somewhat, being 14,500 m (47,570 ft) and 1,170 km (726 miles) respectively; maximum endurance was now 2 hours 6 minutes. The field performance was still good, with a take-off and landing run of 640-630 m (2,100-2,070 ft) and a landing speed of 167 km/h (103 mph).

The tables on pages 33-34 give further details of La-15 '202 White' (c/n 52210202) as recorded during the checkout trials.

Meanwhile, as mentioned earlier, the La-15 achieved initial operational capability,

Weights and CG Positions of La-15 c/n 52210202

Configuration	Weight, kg (lb)	CG position (gear down), % MAC	Nose-over angle during braking
Dry weight	2,575 (5,680)	38.5	n.a.
Normal all-up weight	3,850 (8,490)	24.55	26°
Zero-fuel weight (OEW)	2,950 (6,500)	22.5	25°

Note: The useful load in normal AUW configuration consisted of the following:

Item	Weight, kg (lb)
Pilot	90 (198)
Fuel	900 (1,980)
Engine oil (12 litres/Imp gal)	10 (22)
Armament (3 x NR-23 cannons)	113 (249)
Ammunition (300 rounds)	125 (275)
Removable equipment (oxygen bottle, communications radio transmitter and receiver, direction finder receiver, AC converters for the radio and the DF, Bariy IFF transponder, gun camera)	37 (81)
Total	1,275 (2,810)

Maximum Speed of La-15 c/n 52210202

Altitude, m (ft)	Maximum speed, km/h (mph)	Mach number
0 (sea level)	900 (559) *	0.735
1,000 (3,280)	944 (586) *	0.780
2,000 (6,560)	992 (616) *	0.829
3,000 (9,840)	1,026 (637)	0.867
4,000 (13,120)	1,025 (636)	0.877
5,000 (16,400)	1,023 (635)	0.886
6,000 (19,685)	1,019 (632)	0.895
7,000 (22,965)	1,014 (629)	0.902
8,000 (26,250)	1,007 (625)	0.908
9,000 (29,530)	998 (619)	0.913
10,000 (32,810)	986 (612)	0.914
11,000 (36,090)	969 (601)	0.912

* The speed at these altitudes was restricted by the dynamic pressure limit of 3,900 kg/m² (799.6 lb/sq ft)

Climb Times and Vertical Speeds of La-15 c/n 52210202

Altitude, m (ft)	Continuous climb time, minutes	Vertical speed, m/sec (ft/min): at full military power (14,700 rpm)	at nominal power (14,100 rpm)
0 (sea level)	–	31.7 (6,240)	24.1 (4,740)
1,000 (3,280)	0.6	30.0 (5,900)	22.9 (4,510)
2,000 (6,560)	1.2	28.1 (5,530)	21.6 (4,250)
3,000 (9,840)	1.8	26.3 (5,180)	20.3 (4,000)
4,000 (13,120)	2.5	24.4 (4,800)	18.9 (3,720)
5,000 (16,400)	3.1	22.5 (4,430)	17.5 (3,440)
6,000 (19,685)	4.0	20.5 (4,035)	16.1 (3,170)
7,000 (22,965)	4.9	18.5 (3,640)	14.6 (2,870)
8,000 (26,250)	6.0	n.a.	13.0 (2,560)
9,000 (29,530)	7.4	n.a.	11.4 (2,240)
10,000 (32,810)	9.0	n.a.	9.6 (1,890)
11,000 (36,090)	10.9	n.a.	7.6 (1,500)
12,000 (39,370)	13.5	n.a.	5.3 (1,040)
13,000 (42,650)	18.0	n.a.	2.3 (450)
13,500 (44,290)	23.4	n.a.	0.5 (100)

Optimum Sustained Turn Parameters of La-15 c/n 52210202

Altitude, m (ft)	Indicated airspeed, km/h (mph)	Turn time, seconds	Turn radius, m (ft)	G load
5,000 (16,400)	500 (310)	38.0	1,100 (3,610)	3.28
8,000 (26,250)	480 (298)	53.0	1,660 (5,450)	2.65

Combat Turn (Chandelle) Parameters of La-15 c/n 52210202

Entry altitude, m (ft)	Exit altitude, m (ft)	Altitude change, m (ft)	Entry speed, km/h (mph)	Exit speed, km/h (mph)	Speed change, km/h (mph)	Time, sec
4,750 (15,580)	7,000 (22,965)	2,250 (7,380)	760 (472)	300 (186)	460 (285)	40

Take-Off Performance of La-15 c/n 52210202

AUW, kg (lb)	Flap setting	Engine rpm	Take-off run, m (ft)	Take-off run time, sec	Unstick speed, km/h (mph)	Take-off distance to h=25 m (82 ft), m (ft)
3,780 (8,330)	20°	14,790	640 (2,100)	19.6	225 (139)	1,270 (4,170)

Landing Performance of La-15 c/n 52210202

AUW, kg (lb)	Flap setting	Landing run, m (ft)	Landing roll time, sec	Landing speed, km/h (mph)	Landing distance from h=25 m (82 ft), m (ft)
3,020 (6,660)	58°	630 (2,070)	21.0	167 (103)	1,280 (4,200)

Notes: The parameters were measured on a concrete runway. Braking on landing was done using the wheel brakes only (the airbrakes were not deployed). The data have been calculated for standard conditions with no wind. The stated AUW of 3,780 kg is the weight at the moment of brake release (less the weight of the fuel burned off during engine starting, taxiing and engine run-up at the line-up point. The landing gear was retracted at the end of the initial acceleration on take-off. The landing AUW of 3,020 kg is the weight of the aircraft less ammunition and with enough fuel to circle the airfield at nominal power for five minutes. During the landing approach the engine was running at idling rpm.

Airbrake Efficiency Coefficient for La-15 c/n 52210202

Altitude, m (ft)	Maximum speed, 'clean' (Vmax), km/h (mph)	Maximum speed with airbrakes (VmaxAB), km/h (mph)	Airbrake efficiency coefficient (Vmax/VmaxAB)
5,200 (17,060)	1,038 (644)	753 (467)	1.38

(Note: Airbrake efficiency in level flight can be assessed by comparing the maximum speed in 'clean' configuration and with airbrakes deployed.)

and service tests were going on in the 196th IAP which had previously operated the Yak-15. The new fighter was fast and agile, possessing an excellent rate of climb; it was also well armed and easy to maintain. However, as with any new aircraft type, manufacturing defects inevitably surfaced in the course of intensive trials operation. The most serious ones included unsatisfactory operation of the production RD-500 turbojets at full military power above 8,000-9,000 m (26,250-29,530 ft); the engine was prone to surging and overheating, and cracks appeared in the inlet guide vanes. The main and auxiliary hydraulic systems (the latter served exclusively the aileron actuator) also functioned

unreliably; hydraulic problems included jamming of slide valves due to corrosion and hydraulic pressure drops. As mentioned earlier, the mainwheel tyres and brakes suffered from intensive wear and tear caused by excessive loads, frequently grounding the aircraft for repairs.

While the wheel issue was nothing new (it had come up at the flight test phase, and OKB-301 was already taking corrective measures by designing new and larger mainwheels), the powerplant and hydraulic system defects first manifested themselves in the course of actual operations. Apart from these problems, which affected virtually the entire La-15 fleet, numerous minor defects

kept cropping up on individual aircraft. These included spontaneous flap deflection at high speed due to airflow suction, rupturing of the canopy perimeter seal (an inflatable rubber hose) and ingress of silica gel dust from the cockpit air filter into the cockpit. The manufacturing standard of the early production machines was inevitably lower than that of the prototypes, which were virtually hand-crafted. The production factory's lack of prior experience with jets was undoubtedly a contributing factor, as was the multitude of changes introduced into the fighter's design in the course of production – even though the factory's staff did their best to rectify the faults on new aircraft and the ones already manufactured as quickly as possible.

The manufacturing defects accounted for several accidents and incidents with operational La-15s. The first loss of a production La-15 occurred on 19th April 1949, even before the service trials began. As Maj. A. Zotov was making a practice flight in preparation for the traditional May Day parade, an engine fire broke out, forcing Zotov to make the first-ever ejection in the Soviet Union; the pilot parachuted to safety and was later awarded the Red Star Order for his bravery (and for demonstrating that ejection seats were viable, one might suppose – Auth.). His colleague Lt. Zagorets was less fortunate. Barely six weeks later his La-15 suffered an engine failure; the pilot did his best to save the fighter but was killed in the ensuing forced landing. On 21st July 1949 the 196th IAP's CO, Guards Col. A. P. Shishkin, crashed fatally during an aerobatics session at Kubinka AB; the cause of the crash was never established with certainty. The service trials report states failure of the elevator trim tab control rod as a possible cause, suggesting that the runaway trim tab caused severe vibration of the elevators and that eventually the elevator control rod broke. However, an experiment conducted by TsAGI disproved this – no elevator vibrations were detected when a full-size La-15 with the elevator trim tab control rod disconnected was tested in the T-101 wind tunnel. Yevgeniy G. Pepelyayev, who was then the unit's deputy CO (later he gained fame as one of the Soviet Union's top-scoring Korean War aces and was awarded the HSU title), believed that Shishkin had simply initiated a spin from which he could not recover; fighting to the last to regain control of the aircraft, he ejected too late and his parachute did not open fully.

Speaking of which, spinning trials of the La-15 and the MiG-15 were held by GK NII VVS a while later, with Andrey G. Kochetkov and Yuriy Antipov respectively as project test pilots. The pilots reported that both fighters handled rather oddly at high angles of attack; therefore the spin entry altitude was increased from the original 5,000 m (16,400 ft) to 7,000 m (22,965 ft) for safety's sake. As an additional safety feature, spin recovery rockets were fitted under the wings, two on each side. GK NII VVS was already familiar with these rockets, having used them before during spinning trials of piston-engined aircraft.

The trials showed that both fighters pitched up slightly before entering a spin. This indicated that the La-15 and the MiG-15 were potentially prone to entering a flat spin – a particularly nasty and dangerous variety from which it is hard to recover. This was an inherent weakness of the two fighters' chosen layouts, which featured swept wings (albeit placed differently) combined with a high-set swept horizontal tail. Then the spin entry altitude was further increased to 8,000-10,000 m (26,250-32,810 ft) – a wise decision, as it turned out. On one occasion Kochetkov was very late in initiating spin recovery due to circumstances beyond his control; as a result, the La-15 ('202 White') made nearly ten extra turns in the spin and would not recover until the rockets were ignited.

The trials showed clearly that swept-wing aircraft were much more reluctant to recover from a spin as compared to straight-wing aircraft and required a different recovery technique. It was not enough just to apply opposite rudder and then push the stick forward a quarter of a turn or half a turn later; the pilot had to watch carefully for the moment when the aircraft's yawing motion would start slowing down and push the stick forward at that very moment. The MiG-15 was somewhat more demanding in this respect, requiring the ailerons to be set strictly neutral (hence a thick white line with which the stick had to be aligned was painted down the middle of the instrument panel to assist the pilot during spin recovery).

The abovementioned accident at Kubinka AB was the case where personal relations played their part. Guards Col. A. P. Shishkin was a wartime buddy and protégé of Guards Lt. Gen. Vasiliy I. Stalin, the Soviet leader's son, who was then Commander of the Moscow Military District's Air Force component. On learning of the crash and his friend's demise Stalin Jr. promptly ordered the service trials of the La-15 to be terminated; the surviving aircraft were to be transferred to Air Defence Force units. Thus, even though the pilots of the 196th IAP did fly their La-15s at the Aviation Day flypast at Moscow-Tushino in August 1949, the crash sealed the fighter's fate. That same month, in August, the Powers That Be took the decision to terminate La-15 production in Saratov.

Accident attrition continued in 1950; it seemed that the La-15 was jinxed. Thus, in one of the IA PVO units to which the La-15s had been banished, one of the fighters suffered a failure of the aileron actuator during a turn; a crash landing ensued in which the aircraft was written off. Several more accidents of the same sort occurred shortly afterwards. For example, on 17th April a production La-15 converted into a testbed by LII crashed during

Above: 196th IAP commanding officer Guards Col. A. P. Shishkin. His fatal crash in an La-15 on 21st July 1949 had grave consequences for the type.

a test flight. Two months later the canopy of La-15 '111 White' (c/n 52210111) disintegrated at 6,300 m (20,670 ft), causing decompression. The pilot lost consciousness for a while and the aircraft was damaged beyond repair in the ensuing dead-stick emergency landing. On 2nd October 1950 another La-15 suffered a failure of the Perspex cover enclosing the landing light built into the air intake splitter. Apparently the slipstream entering through the hole overpressurised the avionics bay located ahead of the cockpit and its dorsal access cover was torn off; next, the aircraft

La-15 batches manufactured by plant No.21 were quite large, as indicated by this machine serialled '457 Red' (c/n 52210457); note the 'La-15' badge on the nose typical of Gor'kiy-built examples. This particular aircraft was used in a test programme of some sort.

Above and below: These excellent photos show Saratov-built La-15 '01 Red' (c/n 0103), which underwent checkout trials at GK NII VVS in December 1949; these included operations from a packed snow runway. Note the powder stains on the nose caused by firing the cannons.

entered an uncontrollable dive and broke up in mid-air after exceeding the design speed limit, killing pilot Britousov.

Of course, the defects afflicting the La-15 at the evaluation stage and the accidents involving the type were nothing more than the usual teething troubles encountered with any aircraft entering mass production. Modifications made by OKB-301 and the production plants' own design offices made it possible to improve the reliability of the La-15 to an acceptable level fairly quickly. The new jet fighters' idiosyncrasies revealed by GK NII VVS during trials were duly taken into account by developing new piloting techniques, and revised flight manuals and instructions were distributed to the aircrews in operational units. After that, the surviving La-15s stayed in service until 1954 and showed a reliability and safety record no worse than other contemporary Soviet Air Force aircraft. Yet, due to the prompt decision to terminate production in 1949 the La-15s total production run was a mere 235 aircraft, comprising 189 Gor'kiy-built examples and the 46 examples that were manufactured in Saratov.

In order to assess the manufacturing standard of Saratov-built La-15s, on 3rd January – 28th February 1950 GK NII VVS conducted checkout trials of a La-15 coded '01 Red' (c/n 0103 – that is, 01st aircraft in Batch 03). The trials results are given in the tables below.

In February-March 1950 test pilot S. G. Brovtsev verified the La-15's canopy jettison system. These tests were preceded by a number of test flights with the hinged canopy portion removed in order to determine the speed at which the slipstream entering the open cockpit made piloting unbearable.

Thus, the La-15's brief service career was plagued by a host of problems. On the other hand, the MiG-15's service entry was not

Specifications of La-15 c/n 0103 as Recorded During Checkout Trials

Powerplant	RD-500
All-up weight, kg (lb)	3,865 (8,520)
Fuel capacity, litres (Imp gal)	1,080 (237.6)
Maximum speed, km/h (mph):	
at 3,000 m (9,840 ft)	1,018 (632)
at 8,000 m (26,250 ft)	992 (616)
Climb time, minutes:	
to 5,000 m (16,400 ft)	3.2
to 10,000 m (32,810 ft)	9.5
Rate of climb at sea level, m/sec (ft/min)	31.1 (6,120)
Service ceiling, m (ft)	13,300 (43,635) *
Maximum range at 10,000 m (32,810 ft), km (miles)	1,170 (726)
Maximum endurance at 10,000 m	2 hours 6 minutes †
Take-off run, m (ft)	695 (2,280) ‡
Take-off distance to h=25 m (82 ft), m (ft)	1,990 6,530) ‡
Landing run, m (ft)	700 (2,300) ‡
Landing distance from h=25 m (82 ft), m (ft)	1,240 (4,070) ‡

Notes:

* The service ceiling was determined at nominal power (14,100 rpm) because the production RD-500 was prone to surging at full military power (14,700 rpm) above 8,000-9,000 m (26,250-29,530 ft).

† On internal fuel only.

‡ The field performance was determined on a packed snow runway.

Range and Endurance of La-15 c/n 0103

Altitude, m (ft)	Flight mode	Speed, km/h (mph):		Engine rpm	Results at fuel burnout			
		IAS	TAS		Range, km (miles):		Endurance, hr-min:	
					in level flight	overall	in level flight	overall
1,000 (3,280)	Maximum range	500 (310)	523 (324)	11,400	595 (369)	610 (378)	1-08	1-15
5,000 (16,400)	ditto	450 (279)	569 (353)	12,000	760 (472)	843 (523)	1-19	1-32
10,000 (32,810)	ditto	420 (260)	694 (431)	12,900	965 (599)	1,170 (726)	1-23	1-47
10,000 (32,810)	Maximum endurance	300 (186)	507 (314)	12,300	870 (540)	1,075 (667)	1-42	2-06
12,000 (39,370)	ditto	300 (186)	575 (357)	13,100	760 (472)	1,040 (645)	1-18	1-51

Notes: Take-off weight 3,865 kg (8,520 lb); fuel supply 1,080 litres (237.6 Imp gal); take-off performed at full military power followed by climb at nominal power.

IAS = indicated airspeed; TAS = true airspeed.

The range and endurance calculations take account of the following:

fuel burnoff on the ground (engine run-up and taxying in the course of five minutes);

fuel burnoff, the time required and the distance covered during take-off, climb and descent;

fuel burnoff and the time required to make a circuit of the airfield on landing and perform the final approach.

Fuel Consumption, Climb/Descent Time and Distance Covered During Take-Off, Climb and Descent

Altitude, m (ft)	Take-off at full military power (14,700 rpm), climb at nominal power (14,100 rpm)				Gliding descent to 500 m (1,640 ft), dynamic pressure 1.85 kg/cm² (26.42 lb/sq in)			
	IAS, km/h (mph)	Fuel used, litres (Imp gal)	Time, min	Distance, km (miles)	IAS, km/h (mph)	Fuel used, litres (Imp gal)	Time, min	Distance, km (miles)
1,000 (3,280)	560 (347)	65 (14.3)	2	10 (6.2)	650 (403)	5 (1.1)	1	5 (3.1)
5,000 (16,400)	480 (298)	145 (31.9)	5	45 (28)	650 (403)	15 (3.3)	4	40 (24.8)
10,000 (32,810)	380 (236)	245 (53.9)	12	105 (65)	550 (341)	40 (8.8)	8	100 (62)
12,000 (39,370)	340 (211)	330 (72.6)	19	160 (99)	450 (279)	50 (11)	10	120 74.5)

Note: Take-off weight 3,865 kg (8,520 lb).

exactly smooth either, and the Mikoyan fighter had its fair share of teething troubles. However, the military decided that operating several jet fighter types filling the same role was too much of a logistical headache, so they picked the MiG as the Soviet Air Force's principal fighter. As early as 1953 the Air Force started withdrawing the La-15, and the remaining 154 examples were finally struck off charge in 1954. Most of the airframes ended up as targets at a nuclear test range where they were used to assess the effects of

A selection of stills from a cine film showing the airmen of the 196th IAP taking off from Kubinka AB for the 1949 Aviation Day parade. The aircraft, which sported red noses for the occasion, include '116 White' (c/n 52210116), '117 White' (c/n 52210117), '210 White' (c/n 52210210) and '220 White' (c/n 52210220).

Above left: 196th IAP deputy CO Yevgeniy G. Pepelyayev, the future Korean War ace. He performed solo aerobatics in a La-15 at the 1949 Aviation Day event.
Above right: This picture taken at the parade was one of the first images of the La-15 to be published in the West.

a nuclear blast on military hardware; the removed engines found further use in KS anti-shipping cruise missiles – ironically, designed by the Mikoyan OKB. Fortunately, one La-15 has been preserved for posterity in the Soviet Air Force Museum (now the Central Russian Air Force Museum) in Monino near Moscow.

The La-15 was destined to be the last brainchild of the famous aircraft designer Semyon A. Lavochkin to see production and service – and the only Lavochkin jet aircraft to do so. True, OKB-301 brought out a few more fighter prototypes afterwards, but, unlike their competitors from the Mikoyan stable, they did not leave a significant mark in aviation history. Also, unlike the MiG-15, the La-15 was not used in actual combat, although some Western sources mistakenly reported that the type was used in the Korean War. Nevertheless, the Lavochkin OKB deserves credit for pioneering swept-wing technology in the Soviet Union and creating quite capable fighters designed around virtually every jet engine type available at the time.

The NATO Air Standards Coordinating Committee (ASCC) assigned the reporting name *Fantail* to the La-15. For a while the fighter was erroneously referred to in the West as the La-17 – no doubt an 'abridged' version of the original La-174 designation. (The real La-17 was a turbojet-powered target drone.)

'Aircraft 180' (UTI La-15) Fighter Trainer Prototype

When the government and MAP took the decision to terminate production of the La-15, virtually all further work on tactical fighters at OKB-301 was abandoned. The only exception was the development of a two-seat conversion trainer variant of the La-15. The trainer received the designation 'aircraft 180'.

Two prototypes of the '180' were converted from standard Gor'kiy-built La-15s by OKB-301's prototype construction facility in

Moscow. The trainee's and instructor's cockpits were located in tandem under a common canopy with individual sideways-hinged portions; the instrumentation in both cockpits was virtually identical. The overall length of the aircraft remained unchanged. The installation of the rear cockpit necessitated a reduction in internal fuel capacity to 870 litres (191.4 Imp gal). Additionally, the three NR-23 cannons were replaced by a single 12.7-mm (.50 calibre) Berezin UBK machine-gun with 100 rounds and a spent case collector.

The first prototype was completed in late August 1949, undergoing manufacturer's flight tests between 8th and 29th September; the machine was flown by OKB-301 test pilots A. F. Kosarev and A. V. Davydov. Since the designers had succeeded in keeping the trainer's all-up weight within the limits specified for the production single-seater, the aircraft's rate of climb and field performance were almost identical to those of the standard La-15. On the other hand, because of the new canopy's greater cross-section area and hence higher drag the maximum speed of the '180' was reduced to 980 km/h (608 mph) at 3,000-4,000 m (9,840-13,120 ft). Since the trainer was powered by an early-production RD-500 which, as already mentioned, was prone to surging at full military power (14,700 rpm) at altitudes in excess of 8,000 m (26,250 ft), the service ceiling had to be established at nominal power (14,100 rpm); it was 12,750 m (41,830 ft). Range on internal fuel at 10,000 m (32,810 ft) was reduced to 910 km (565 miles). As regards stability and handling, the '180' trainer was broadly similar to the production single-seat La-15. The first prototype underwent state acceptance trials at GK NII VVS between December 1949 and February 1950.

The second prototype was completed and joined the trials programme shortly afterwards; yet, considering that the baseline La-15 was out of production by then, there

Top and centre: Two stills from Pepelyayev's solo aerobatics display over Tushino.

Above: A trio of red-nosed La-15s makes a formation turn at the 1949 event.

was no point in launching production of the trainer. After the trials both two-seaters were delivered to first-line La-15 units, receiving the service designation UTI La-15 (or La-15UTI – *oochebno-trenirovochnyy istrebitel'*, training fighter), by analogy with the UTI MiG-15.

Above left: Front view of the first prototype of the '180' (UTI La-15) trainer, showing the larger canopy cross-section, the offset aerial mast and the lack of the landing/taxi light built into the air intake splitter.

Left and below left: Two more views of the first prototype, showing the shape of the new canopy enclosing the tandem cockpits. Note the bulges on the main gear doors to accommodate the larger mainwheels.

Above and right: The '180' seen during state acceptance trials. Note the retractable landing/taxi light ahead of the port mainwheel well.

Below: Though outwardly a standard La-15, '415 Blue' (c/n 52210415) was an aerodynamics research aircraft. The machine was lost in a crash on 17th April 1950.

Lavochkin OKB test pilot A. F. Kosarev was one of the two pilots who tested the '180' trainer.

La-15 Aerodynamics Research Aircraft

A production La-15 serialled '415 Blue' (c/n 52210415) was converted into an aerodynamics research aircraft with a system of vents on the wings and tail unit. Unfortunately this aircraft crashed on 17th April 1950, diving into the ground five minutes after take-off from Zhukovskiy on a test mission; test pilot A. M. Yershov was killed.

La-15 Landing Gear Testbed

In 1950 another production La-15 was converted into a testbed for verifying some of the systems developed for the Lavochkin OKB's 'aircraft 190' all-weather interceptor (see Chapter 6). In particular, the standard tricycle landing gear was replaced by an experimental bicycle landing gear with outrigger struts under the wingtips. Test pilot A. V. Davydov managed to make several flights in this aircraft but on 12th June an accident occurred at the beginning of yet another test mission. As had been the case on previous occasions, Davydov retracted the outrigger struts even before the aircraft reached unstick speed; then the machine suddenly banked and yawed. This had occurred in previous flights; this time, however, all attempts to level the wings proved fruitless and the pilot did the only possible thing, aborting the take-off. As the fighter sank back on the runway, the nose gear unit collapsed and the La-15 veered off the runway, colliding with a modified Tupolev Tu-2 piston-engined bomber used as a testbed. Luckily the results of the collision were limited to a damaged tail on the bomber and a shattered canopy on the fighter; the pilot had a close call but was unhurt. The cause of the accident was never established, but a burst tyre was viewed as the most likely cause.

Basic Specifications of the La-15 Family

	'174'	'174D'	La-15 c/n 52210202 (Gor'kiy-built)	La-15 c/n 0103 (Saratov-built)	'180' (first prototype)
	Manufacturer's flight tests	State acceptance trials	State checkout trials	Special checkout trials	Manufacturer's flight tests
Powerplant	RR Derwent V	RR Derwent V	RD-500	RD-500	RD-500
Empty weight, kg (lb)	n.a.	2,433 (5,363)	2,575 (5,680)	n.a.	2,805 (6,180)
All-up weight, kg (lb)	3,600 (7,940)	3,708 (8,174)	3,850 (8,490)	3,865 (8,520)	3,730 (8,220)
Fuel capacity, litres (Imp gal)	n.a.	1,110 (244.2)	1,060 (233.2)	1,080 (237.6)	870 (191.4)
Maximum speed, km/h (mph)					
at altitude	1,038 (644)	1,040 (646)	1,026 (637)	1,018 (632)	980 (608)
	4,000 (13,120)	3,000 (9,840)	3,000 (9,840)	3,000 (9,840)	3,000-4,000 (9,840-13,120)
Maximum speed at 8,000 m (26,250 ft), km/h (mph)	1,004 (623)	1,020 (633)	1,007 (625)	992 (616)	948 (588)
Climb time, minutes:					
to 5,000 m (16,400 ft)	2.8	3.0	3.1	3.2	3.0
to 10,000 m (32,810 ft)	7.0	9.2	9.0	9.5	9.3
Rate of climb at sea level, m/sec (ft/min)	n.a.	33.0 (6,490)	31.7 (6,240)	31.1 (6,120)	32.8 (6,455)
Service ceiling, m (ft)	n.a.	14,600 (47,900)	13,500 (44,290) *	13,300 (43,635) *	12,750 (41,830)
Maximum range at 10,000 m, km (miles)	1,220 (757)	1,300 (807)	1,145 (711)	1,170 (726)	910 (565)
Maximum endurance at 10,000 m †	1 hr 56 min	2 hrs 28 min	1 hr 59 min	2 hrs 6 min	1 hr 30 min
360° turn time at 5,000 m, sec	n.a.	37.5	38.0	n.a.	n.a.
Altitude gain in a combat turn at 5,000 m, m (ft)	n.a.	2,350 (7,710)	2,250 (7,380)	n.a.	n.a.
Take-off run, m (ft) ‡	590 (1,935)	595 (1,950)	640 (2,100)	695 (2,280)	n.a.
Take-off distance, m (ft) ‡	n.a.	1,370 (4,490)	1,270 (4,170)	1,990 6,530)	n.a.
Landing run, m (ft) ‡	400 (1,310)	550 (1,800)	630 (2,070)	700 (2,300)	n.a.
Landing distance, m (ft) ‡	n.a.	1,050 (3,440)	1,280 (4,200)	1,240 (4,070)	n.a.
Armament	3 x 23-mm cannons 300 rounds	3 x 23-mm cannons 300 rounds	3 x 23-mm cannons 300 rounds	3 x 23-mm cannons 300 rounds	1 x 12.7-mm machine gun 100 rounds

Notes:

* The service ceiling of the production La-15s and the '180-1' was determined at nominal power (14,100 rpm) because the production RD-500 was prone to surging at full military power (14,700 rpm) above 8,000-9,000 m (26,250-29,530 ft)

† On internal fuel only

‡ The field performance was determined on a packed snow runway

Chapter 4

The La-15 in Detail

Type: Single-engined tactical fighter designed for operation in visual meteorological conditions (VMC).

Fuselage: Semi-monocoque all-metal stressed-skin structure with 25 frames, four longerons and a set of stringers supporting the skin whose thickness varies from 1 to 1.5 mm (0.039 to 0.059 in). The riveted fuselage structure is made mainly of D-16 duralumin; steel is used for the attachment fittings.

Structurally the fuselage consists of two sections: forward (up to the dual frame 14, which is the fuselage break point) and rear. The latter is detachable for engine maintenance and removal; the two fuselage sections are held together by 56 bolts.

The *forward fuselage* incorporates the avionics/equipment bay (frames 1-3), the nosewheel well (frames 1-5), the cockpit, the cannon bay aft of it and the mainwheel wells (frames 8-12). The Nos 1 and 2 bag-type fuel tanks are located between the wheel wells, with the rigid service tank below them (frames

8-11). The circular air intake with a detachable annular nose fairing affixed to frame 1 has a vertical splitter which divides it into two elliptical-section air ducts passing along the fuselage sides, flanking the avionics bay, cockpit, nosewheel well and fuel tanks.

The forward fuselage structure includes the four longerons (located in the cockpit area) and six mainframes absorbing the main structural loads. Mainframe No.1 carries the nose landing gear unit; attachment fittings for the wings' forward auxiliary spar, main spar and rear auxiliary spar are installed at mainframes 8, 10 and 11 respectively, while the dual mainframe 10 also carries the main landing gear retraction actuators. Frame 12 mounts the main gear fulcrums and the flap actuator, while frame 14 carries the engine bearer with the engine's forward (main) attachment points. Frames 7-9 are cut away from below and the contour is closed by matching formers Nos 7B, 8 and 9. Dorsal maintenance hatches are provided between frames 8-10, 10-11 and 12-14.

The pressurised cockpit is contained by pressure bulkheads (frames 3 and 7) and the pressure floor. It is enclosed by a two-piece bubble canopy. The fixed windshield consists of a wraparound Perspex rear section 10 mm (0.39 in) thick and an elliptical optically-flat bulletproof windscreen 105 mm (4.13 in) thick. The rear portion of canopy hinges open to starboard; its blown Perspex glazing is 8 mm (0.31 in) thick and incorporates a direct vision window. The canopy can be locked both from within and from the outside and can be jettisoned manually in an emergency by means of a lever on the starboard side.

The cockpit features an ejection seat (with guide rails attached to the rear pressure bulkhead), an instrument panel and side control consoles. Armour protection for the pilot is provided by a forward armour plate 6 mm (0.23 in) thick and the bulletproof windscreen, as well as a rear armour plate and an armoured seat headrest, both of which are 8 mm (0.31 in) thick.

This overall view of the La-15 at the Central Russian Air Force Museum shows the circular-section fuselage. The ventral fin appears to be damaged.

43

Above: This view of the same aircraft shows the asymmetrical placement of the cannons (one to port and two to starboard). Interestingly, the La-15 appears to sit higher on its undercarriage in this view. The air intake is blanked off by a cover.

This view shows the air intake splitter incorporating a landing/taxi light and static ports. The avionics bay cover ahead of the windshield is visible. The car parked alongside is an APA-7 ground power unit based on a Moskvich-400/422 van.

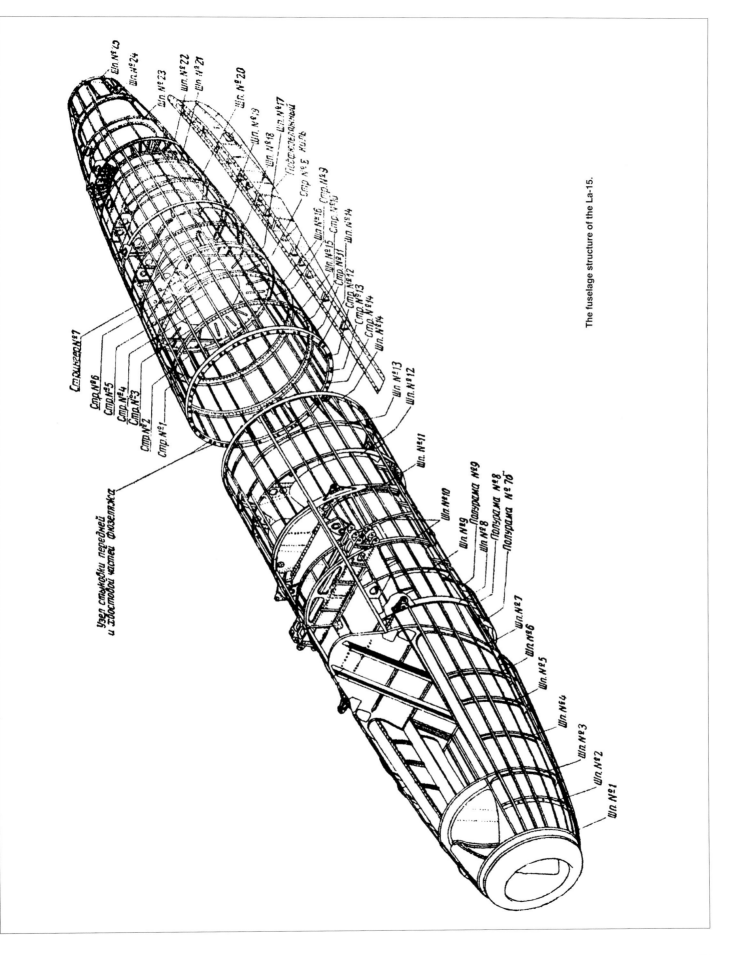

The fuselage structure of the La-15.

45

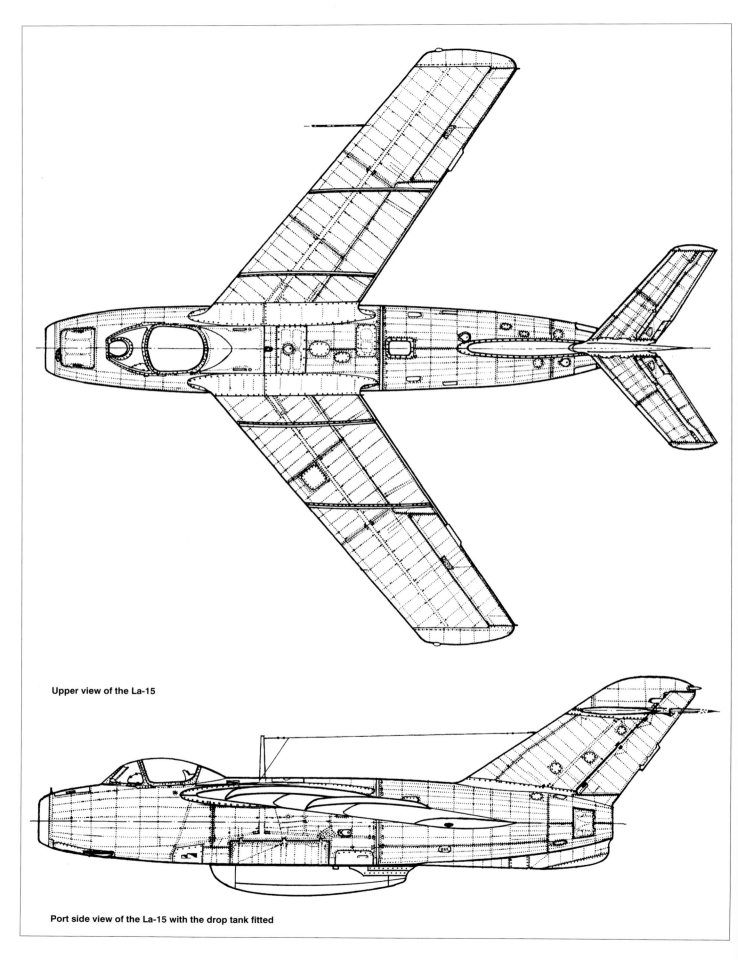

Upper view of the La-15

Port side view of the La-15 with the drop tank fitted

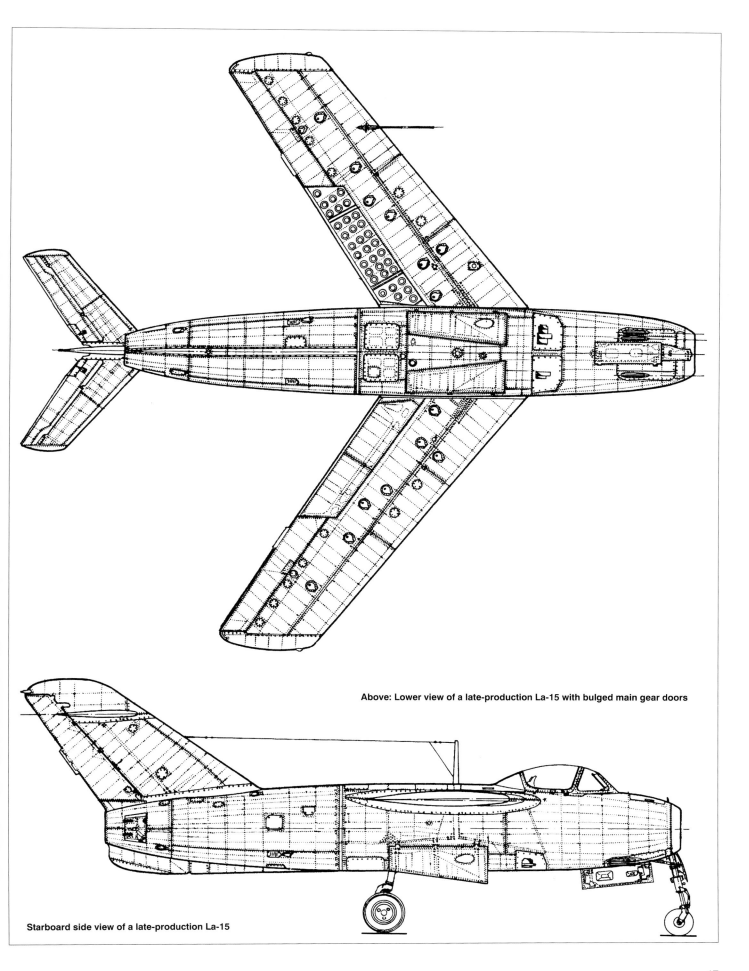

Above: Lower view of a late-production La-15 with bulged main gear doors

Starboard side view of a late-production La-15

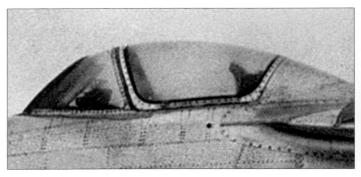

Above: Two views of the canopy of a production La-15's cockpit canopy, showing the thickness of the bulletproof windscreen. The gunsight is visible in the right-hand photo. Note the wraparound glazing of the fixed windshield instead of the usual sidelights (the windscreen frame is not connected to the rear frame).

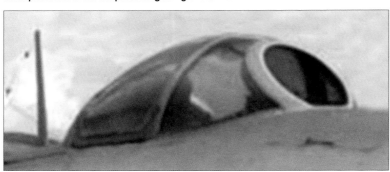

Above: Two more views of the canopy, showing the direct vision window on the port side of the fixed windshield.

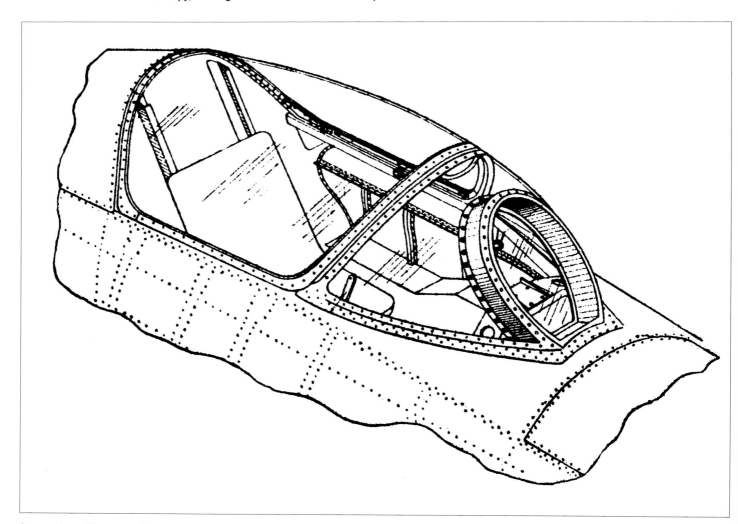

A scrap view of the canopy from the La-15's structural design manual, showing the ejection seat tracks on the cockpit's rear pressure bulkhead.

The *rear fuselage* (frames 14-25) houses the engine with its accessories and jetpipe, the annual integral fuel tank No.3 and control linkages. The rear fuselage structure consists of 15 frames and 28 stringers (1L-14L and 1R-14R) supporting the skin; the front end of each stringer carries an attachment fitting with two bolt holes for mating the fuselage sections. Frame 17 is a bulkhead with attachment fittings for the engine's rear end. Mainframes 19 and 22 feature attachment fittings for the fin's front and rear spars.

Two lateral airbrakes are located between frames 23-24. The airbrakes are hydraulically actuated; they are hinged at the trailing edge, opening rearward like air scoops.

Wings: Cantilever shoulder-mounted monoplane wings. Sweepback at quarter-chord 37°20', anhedral 6°, incidence 1°, aspect ratio 4.82, taper 1.5. The wings utilise the TsAGI 10035M airfoil at the root, the TsAGI 12035M airfoil at ribs 9L/9R and the TsAGI P2-2M airfoil from ribs 12L/12R to the tips; the mean thickness/chord ratio is 12%. Wingspan is 8.83 m (28 ft 11⁴¹⁄₆₄ in) and wing area 16.167 m² (173.83 sq ft).

The wings are of all-metal, three-spar stressed-skin construction, with forward auxiliary spar, main spar and rear auxiliary spar, plus 29 ribs. The skin is made of duralumin and V-95 aluminium alloy. The wings are built in three sections, with one-piece outer wings joined to the centre section, which is integral with the fuselage. The wing/fuselage joint is covered by a fillet attached by screws and anchor nuts.

Each wing has two boundary layer fences riveted to the upper surface. A jacking point is provided on each wing's main spar between ribs 6 and 7.

The wings have one-piece area-increasing flaps terminating at approximately half-span, with one-piece ailerons outboard of these. The flaps are riveted structures with stamped internal structural elements; they are located between the root rib and rib 17 and are attached to ribs 8 and 16. The flaps are hydraulically actuated; there are three flap settings (fully retracted, 20° for take-off and 58° for landing). To prevent spontaneous deflection at high speed the flaps are secured in the retracted position by mechanical uplocks via rubber dampers. Overall flap area is 2.028 m² (21.8 sq ft).

The ailerons are both aerodynamically balanced and mass-balanced, with two lead weights built into the leading edge; they are carried on three brackets located near ribs 17 and 28 and at rib 22. Overall aileron area is 2.024 m² (21.76 sq ft).

Tail unit: Cantilever cruciform tail surfaces of all-metal stressed-skin construction. Both

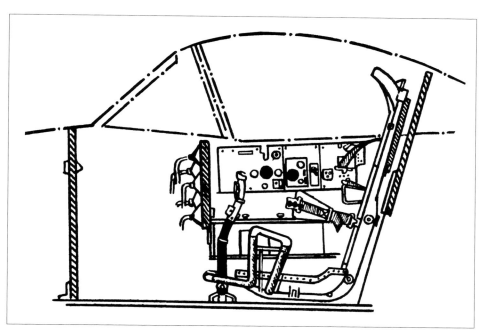

Above: This drawing from the manual shows the position of the pressure bulkheads, the ejection seat, the instrument panel and the control stick.

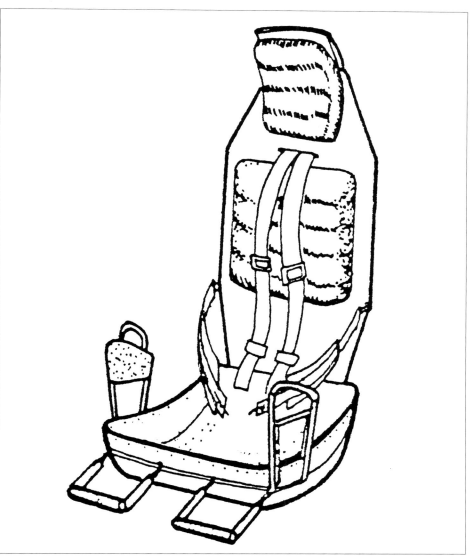

The La-15's ejection seat with a dished seat pan to take the pilot's parachute, with padded back- and headrests and leg supports. The ejection handle is located on the starboard side.

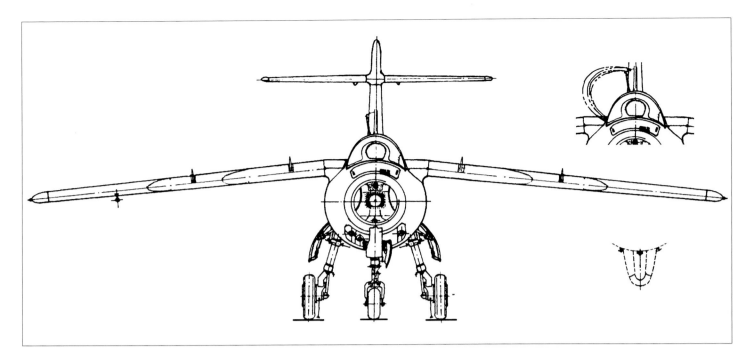

Above: Front view of a production La-15, with a scrap view of the open cockpit canopy. The other scrap view is a front view of the drop tank.

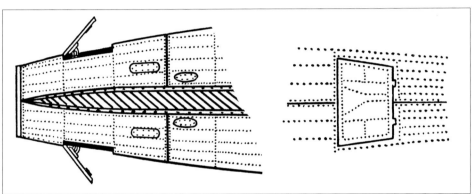

Left: The La-15's airbrakes were aft-hinged, opening like air scoops to create quite a strong drag in spite of their small size.

Below: The port wing of a La-15. The boundary layer fences were of unequal height.

Bottom: This view shows the wings' virtually constant chord and the position of the boundary layer fences with respect to the root rib and the aileron.

horizontal and vertical tail surfaces utilise symmetrical TsAGI V series airfoils.

The *vertical tail* consists of a detachable fin, a one-piece rudder and a shallow ventral strake running the full length of the rear fuselage section. The three-spar fin is attached to the fuselage by two fittings. It is built in two unequal portions to facilitate installation of the horizontal tail and has a forward auxiliary spar, a main spar and a rear auxiliary spar, 15 ribs in the lower section, and two ribs and six webs in the upper section.

The rudder is a single-spar structure with 14 ribs; it is aerodynamically balanced and mass-balanced. The rudder is carried on a two brackets and an axle/lower support.

The *horizontal tail* consists of two stabilisers joined together at the centreline and one-piece elevators. Sweepback at quarter-chord 40°, stabiliser span 2.96 m (9 ft 8¹⁷⁄₃₂ in), horizontal tail area 2.55 m² (27.41 sq ft). Normal incidence is 0°; however, the forward stabiliser attachment fitting is ground-adjustable, allowing the incidence to be varied within +1°/–2°. The stabilisers are single-spar structures with 13 ribs each.

Each elevator is a single-spar structure carried on three brackets and incorporates a trim tab at the inboard end. The elevators have aerodynamic and mass balancing.

Landing gear: Hydraulically retractable tricycle type; wheel track 1.7 m (5 ft 6¹⁵⁄₁₆ in), wheelbase 4.21 m (13 ft 9¾ in). The aft-retracting castoring nose unit attached to fuselage frame 1 is fitted with a single 400 x 150 mm (15.74 x 5.9 in) non-braking wheel carried in a fork. The extended nose gear strut is inclined forward.

The main units mounted on fuselage frame 12 retract forward into the fuselage and have single 570 x 140 mm (22.4 x 5.5 in) wheels equipped with brakes. Steering on the ground is by differential braking. All three units have oleo-pneumatic shock absorbers.

The nosewheel well is closed by a forward door segment attached to the oleo and a lateral door hinged on the port side, the main-wheel wells by one-piece doors hinged along the upper edge. All doors remain open when the gear is down.

Top right: The La-15's starboard wing carries an L-shaped pitot.

Above right: The starboard wingtip fairing and starboard navigation light.

Right: A drawing from the structural manual showing the design of the detachable small upper section of the fin with two horizontal ribs and six webs, the rearmost one being parallel to the rudder leading edge. The upper fin section carries the tail navigation light. The joint between the upper and lower fin is covered by a strip of metal attached by screws.

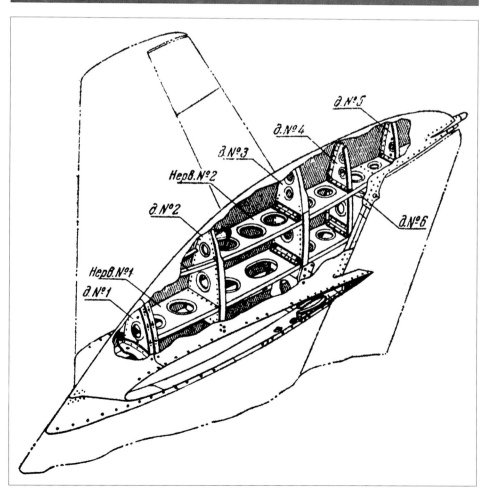

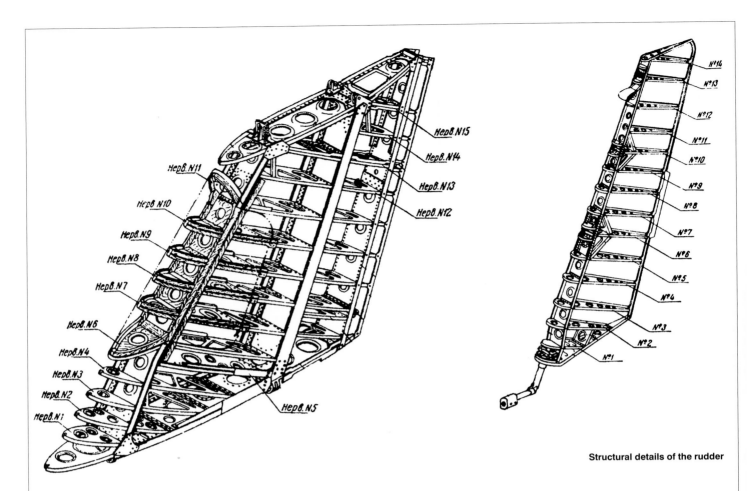

Structural details of the rudder

Structural details of the lower fin section. Note the cranked forward ends of ribs 6 and 11.

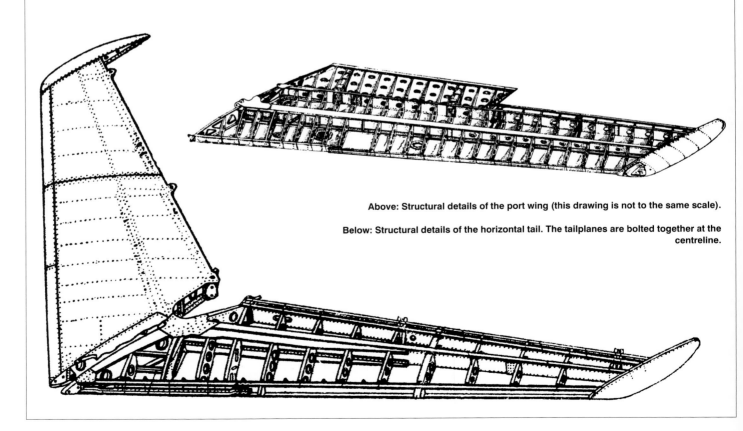

Above: Structural details of the port wing (this drawing is not to the same scale).

Below: Structural details of the horizontal tail. The tailplanes are bolted together at the centreline.

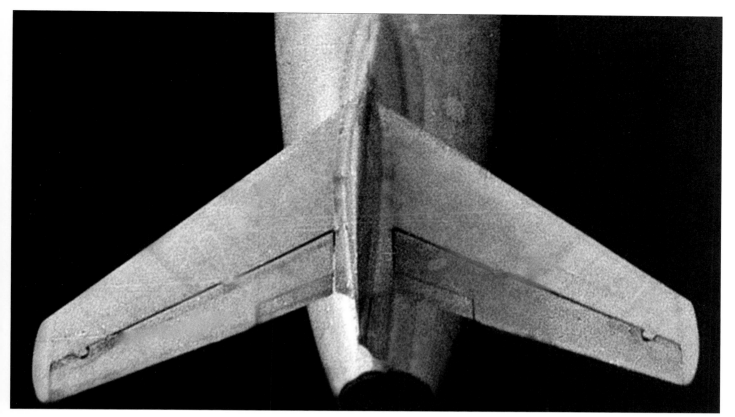

Powerplant: One Klimov RD-500 non-after-burning turbojet with a take-off thrust of 1,590 kgp (3,500 lbst) at 14,700 rpm. The RD-500 is a single-shaft turbojet featuring a single-stage centrifugal compressor (with dual inlet ducts), nine straight-flow combustion chambers, a single-stage axial turbine, a subsonic fixed-area nozzle and an extension jetpipe. The latter is attached flexibly. The engine features a forward-mounted accessory gearbox for driving fuel, oil and hydraulic pumps and electrical equipment. Starting is electrical.

Engine pressure ratio 4.0; mass flow at take-off 28.5 kg/sec (62.83 lb/sec). Turbine temperature 1,130° K. Specific fuel consumption at take-off power 1.05 kg/kgp·hr (lb/lbst·hr).

Top: The horizontal tail of the '174D' prototype. The elevator trim tabs are clearly visible. Note the fin/stabiliser fairings.

Above: The tail unit of a Gor'kiy-built production La-15, showing the rudder hinge brackets and the radio aerial cable attached to the leading edge. The rivet lines on the detachable upper fin section show the location of the vertical webs.

Right: Another view of a production La-15's tail unit. The position of the star insignia with respect to the horizontal tail on different examples varied, as these photos show.

Left: Another view of the tail unit. Note the rudder mass balance in a cutout of the upper fin section.

Below left: The main landing gear units of an early-production La-15 with the original small wheels, as indicated by the smooth wheel well doors.

Below: The nose gear unit is inclined forward.

Right and far right: The main gear units of a late La-15 with larger wheels. Note the parallel grooves in the tyre tread (instead of the early diamonds) and the port side ground power receptacle.

Above: The main gear units of a late-production La-15 featuring larger wheels and bulged wheel well doors. Note the different design of the wheel discs.
Above right: This view of the nose gear shows the recesses in the larger wheel well door for the wheel and the torque link.

Right: A drawing from the structural design manual showing the main gear details.

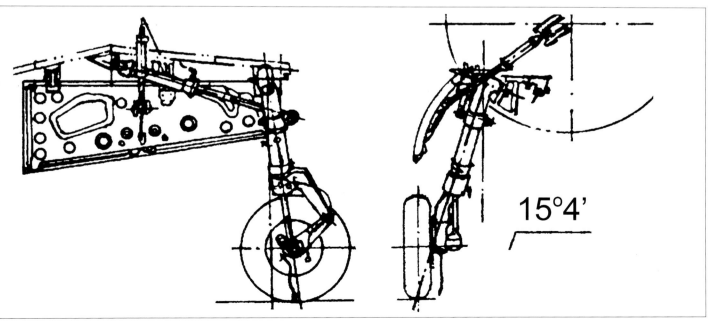

15°4'

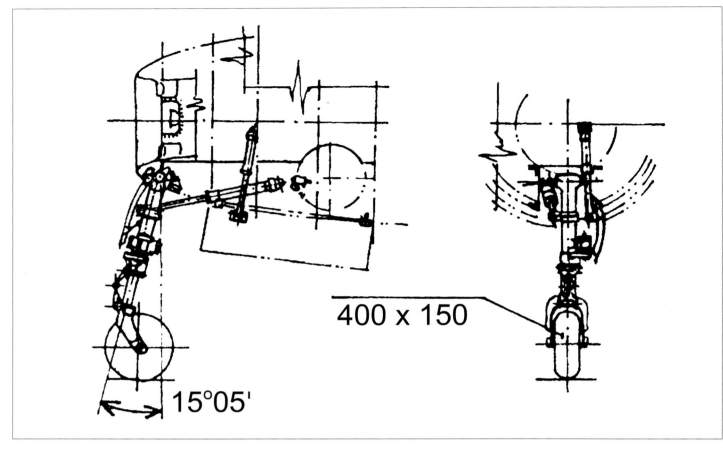

400 x 150

15°05'

Another drawing from the manual detailing the kinematics of the nose gear unit.

Length overall 2,248 mm (7 ft 4½ in); maximum diameter 1,042 mm (3 ft 5 in). Dry weight 567 kg (1,250 lb). Design life 100 hours.

The engine is mounted on a bearer via four attachment points: two trunnions on the right and left sides of the compressor casing below the axis of the engine and two mounting lugs in the upper part of the engine. The engine is attached to fuselage frame 14; when the rear fuselage is detached, the engine is completely exposed.

Control system: Conventional mechanical flight control system. The control rods and cables are provided with rubber pressure seals where they pass through the cockpit's rear pressure bulkhead at frame 7.

Roll control is provided by one-piece ailerons actuated by means of push-pull rods, control cranks and levers. The aileron control circuit includes a hydraulic actuator located aft of the cockpit to reduce the stick forces; this actuator may be switched off by the pilot. The aileron control circuit also features an artificial-feel unit creating a force of 2-2.5 kgf (4.4-5.5 lbf) with the stick fully deflected. Aileron deflection limits are ±16°.

Directional control is provided by a one-piece rudder which is actuated by a system of cables and rollers. The rudder deflection limits are ±25°.

Pitch control is provided by one-piece elevators controlled by means of push-pull rods, cranks and levers. Deflection limits are 30°30' up and 18°30' down. The elevators incorporate electrically actuated trim tabs with a deflection limit of ±14°.

Fuel system: Internal fuel is carried in two bladder tanks housed in the forward fuselage and an annular integral tank in the rear fuselage, from which the fuel is fed to a rigid service tank located below the bladder tanks and thence to the engine. Total internal fuel capacity is 1,100 litres (242 Imp gal), though some documents state 1,060 litres (233.2 Imp gal).

The fuel system includes an electric transfer pump located below the service tank, pipelines (with connectors at frames 12 and 17 allowing the rear fuselage to be detached), fuel metering sensors, an air sensor, a fuel filter, shut-off and defuelling cocks. The tanks are equipped with a vent system.

A 'wet' hardpoint on the fuselage centre-line provides for the carriage of a teardrop-shaped conformal drop tank. The drop tank is pressurised by engine bleed air.

Refuelling is done by gravity via three filler caps – one for the bladder tanks, one for the rear fuselage tank and one on the drop tank. The fuel grade used is Soviet T-1 jet fuel.

Electrics: 28.5 V DC electrical system with a 1.5-kW GSK-1500 engine-driven generator as the main power source. Backup DC power is provided by a 12A-10 (28 V, 10 A.h) silver-zinc battery in the avionics/equipment bay. The generator works with the RK-1500A voltage regulator and the SF-1 filter and is provided with a special air cooling system. A ground power receptacle is provided aft of the port mainwheel well.

Air conditioning and pressurisation system: The La-15 has a ventilation-type cockpit pressurised by engine bleed air to a pressure differential of 0.3 bars (4.28 psi), which is maintained from 7,000-8,000 m (22,965-26,250 ft) upwards. The air is supplied via a heat-insulated pipeline, a filter, a reverse-flow valve and a shut-off cock. Cockpit air pressure is governed automatically by an RD-2I pressure regulator (*regoolyator davleniya*); if this fails, a KADD dual-action automatic safety valve (*klapan-avtomaht dvoynovo deystviya*) prevents overpressurisation. The canopy perimeter is sealed by an inflatable rubber hose pressurised to 2-2.5 bars (28.5-35.7 psi).

Oxygen system: The oxygen equipment includes a KP-14 breathing apparatus (*kislorodnyy pribor*), a 12-litre (2.64 Imp gal) oxygen bottle and a charging connector. The

Above: The Klimov RD-500 centrifugal-flow turbojet powered several Soviet fighter types, including the La-15.

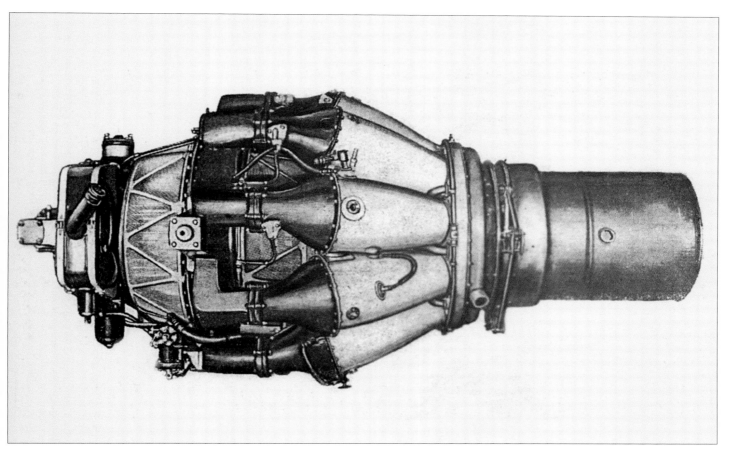

This picture of the RD-500 was included in the La-15's structural manual.

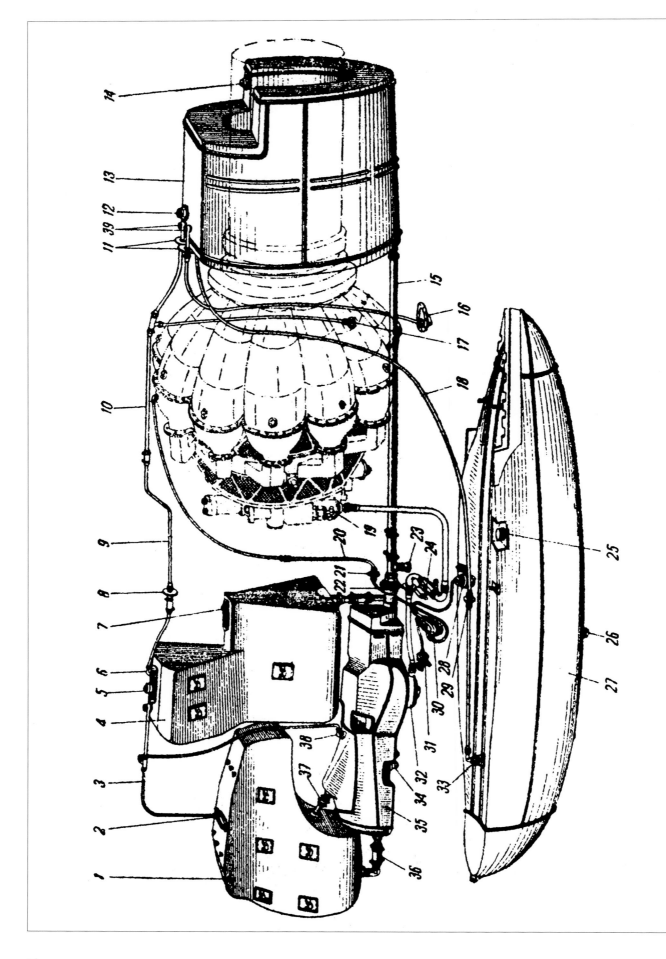

The fuel system layout of the La-15. 1: Forward bladder tank; 2, 6, 38, 39: Vent system connectors; 3, 9, 10: Vent system piping; 4: Centre bladder tank; 5, 12, 25: Filler caps; 7, 14: Fuel quantity meters; 8, 21, 29: Pipeline connectors at fuselage frame 12; 11: Pipeline connectors at fuselage frame 17; 13: Aft integral tank; 15, 36, 37: Fuel transfer pipelines; 16, 17: Vents; 18: Fuel line from drop tank; 19: Engine-mounted low-pressure fuel filter; 20: Air pipeline; 22: Backflow valve; 23: Defuelling cock; 24: Shutoff cock; 26, 34: Defuelling plugs; 27: Drop tank; 28: Air detector; 30: Pressure reduction valve; 31: Pressure sensor; 32: Low-pressure fuel pump; 33: Drop tank connector; 35: Rigid service tank.

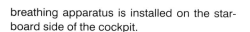

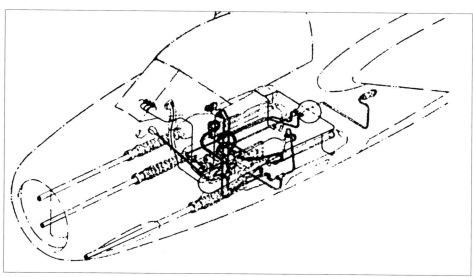

**Above: This drawing from the manual shows the placement of the cannons and their ammunition boxes.
Left and above left: The muzzles of the three NR-23 cannons; the cutouts are surrounded by blast plates.**

breathing apparatus is installed on the starboard side of the cockpit.

Fire suppression system: A fire extinguisher bottle charged with carbon dioxide is installed in the forward fuselage. In the event of engine fire a flame sensor triggers a fire warning light in the cockpit and activates a pyrotechnic valve, letting the gas out into a manifold. The pilot can also activate the system manually.

Avionics and equipment:
Navigation equipment: The navigation equipment was standard for Soviet fighters of the day and included an RPKO-10M direction finder (***rahdiopolukompas***).

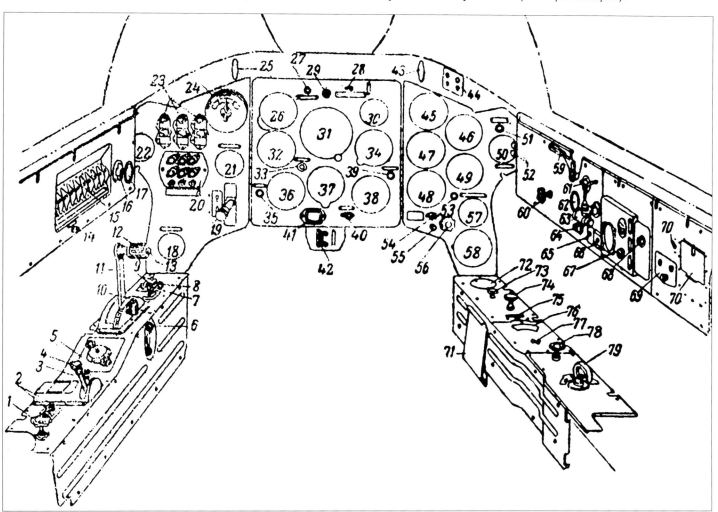

A drawing from the manual showing the location of the instruments and controls in the La-15's cockpit.

Above: The instrument panel of the first prototype La-15 ('aircraft 174'). The basic flight instruments are grouped in the middle; note that one of them is still missing. The right-hand section of the instrument panel carries the engine instruments (exhaust gas temperature gauge, oil temperature gauge and so on). The white handle on the left-hand section of the instrument panel is the landing gear selector; to the left of it is the gear position indicator, with hydraulic system pressure gauges and warning lights above it and the cockpit lighting adjustment knob below it. The gunsight is just visible.

Above right: Overall view of the cockpit of the '174', showing the port cockpit console carrying the throttle. The instrumentation was rather basic.

Right: The starboard cockpit console of the '174' carried the control panel for the radio set and the switches for various ancillary systems.

Left: The trainee's cockpit of the 'aircraft 180' (UTI La-15) trainer was almost identical to that of the production single-seater, showing visible differences from the '174' prototype. The large handle on the right is the canopy jettison handle. Note the direct vision window on the left.

Basic Specifications of the La-15

Powerplant	1 x RD-500
Thrust, kgp (lbst)	1,590 (3,500)
Length overall	9.563 m (31 ft 4½ in)
Fuselage length	8.235 m (27 ft 0 in)
Height on ground	3.8 m (12 ft 5³⁄₆₄ in)
Wing span	8.83 m (28 ft 11⅝ in)
Wing area, m² (sq ft)	16.167 (173.83)
Wing sweep at quarter-chord	37°20'
Wing aspect ratio	4.82
Wing taper	1.5
Root chord	2.207 m (7 ft 2⁵⁷⁄₆₄ in)
Tip chord	1.469 m (4 ft 9⁵³⁄₆₄ in)
Mean aerodynamic chord (MAC)	1.862 m (6 ft 1¹¹⁄₆₄ in)
Flap span	4.94 m (16 ft 2³⁄₆₄ in)
Flap area (total), m² (sq ft)	2.028 (21.8)
Aileron area (total), m² (sq ft)	2.024 (21.76)
Wing thickness/chord ratio	12%
Wing anhedral	6°
Wing incidence	1°
Horizontal tail span	2.96 m (9 ft 8¹⁷⁄₃₂ in)
Horizontal tail sweep at quarter-chord	40°
Horizontal tail aspect ratio	3.44
Horizontal tail taper	2.44
Horizontal tail incidence	0°
Horizontal tail area, m² (sq ft)	2.55 (27.41)
Elevator area (effective), m² (sq ft)	0.84 (9.0)
Elevator trim tab area (total), m² (sq ft)	0.0748 (0.8)
Elevator balance area (total), m² (sq ft)	0.0548 (0.589)
Vertical tail area, m² (sq ft)	3.378 (36.32)
Vertical tail angle relative to aircraft axis	0°
Rudder area (overall), m² (sq ft)	0.89 (9.56)
Rudder balance area, m² (sq ft)	0.1108 (1.19)
Ventral strake area, m² (sq ft)	0.575 (6.18)
Aileron deflection	±16°
Flap settings	
take-off	20°
landing	58°
Elevator deflection:	
up	30°30'
down	18°30'
Elevator trim tab deflection	±14°
Rudder deflection	±25°
Control stick travel:	
forward	13°30'
aft	24°
left/right	±21°
Rudder pedal maximum deflection	26°
Landing gear track	1.7 m (5 ft 6¹⁵⁄₁₆ in)
Landing gear wheelbase	4.21 m (13 ft 9¾ in)
Dry weight, kg (lb)	2,575 (5,680)
Normal take-off weight, kg (lb)	3,850 (8,490)
Empty weight, kg (lb)	2,950 (6,500)
Fuel capacity, litres (Imp gal)	1,060 (233.2)
Maximum speed, km/h (mph):	
at sea level	900 (559)
at high altitude	1,026 (637)
Effective range, km (miles)	1,170 (726)
Rate of climb, m/sec (ft/min)	31.7 (6,240)
Service ceiling, m (ft)	13,500 (44,290)
Armament	3 x 23-mm cannons w. 300 rounds
Crew	1

Communications equipment: RSIU-3 Klyon two-way VHF radio (RSI-6M receiver and RSI-6K transmitter) in the avionics/equipment bay with whip aerial installed on the right side aft of the cockpit. An EKSR-39 signal flare launcher is installed on the starboard side of the rear fuselage.

Flight instrumentation: The flight instrumentation included a KUS-1200 airspeed indicator (ASI, *kombineerovannyy ookazahtel' skorosti*), a VD-15 altimeter, a UVPD-3 cabin altitude/pressure indicator (*ookazahtel' vysoty i perepahda davleniya*), a VS-46 altitude warning device (*vysotnyy signalizahtor*), a DF indicator, M-46 Mach meter and so on.

IFF equipment: SRO-1 Bariy-M IFF transponder with dorsal or ventral blade aerial on the aft fuselage.

Exterior lighting: BANO-45 port and starboard navigation lights at wingtips, tail navigation light on fin tailing edge, FS-155 landing/taxi light in air intake splitter.

Reconnaissance equipment: An AFA-IM reconnaissance camera (*aerofotoapparaht – aerial camera*) covered by a hinged door is installed on the port side of the rear fuselage.

Armament: The La-15 is armed with three 23-mm (.90 calibre) Nudelman/Rikhter NR-23 cannons (one to port and two to starboard) with 100 rounds per gun. Recharging is by recoil action, which allows the heavy-calibre cannons to have a high rate of fire and be relatively lightweight. The NR-23 weighs 39 kg (86 lb) and fires 200-gram (7.06-oz.) projectiles; rate of fire is 800-950 rpm and muzzle velocity 680 m/sec (2,231 ft/sec). Initial charging is done by a pneumatic mechanism operating at 30 bars (428.5 psi).

Firing is controlled electrically. The cannons use fragmentation/incendiary/traced and armour-piercing/incendiary/traced rounds. All cannons are belt-fed; belt links and ammunition cases are discarded during firing.

The first production La-15s manufactured in 1949 had an ASP-1N computing gunsight; on later aircraft this was replaced with an ASP-3N computing gunsight. An S-13 gun camera mounted on the air intake upper lip records the shooting results. The gun camera can operate independently from the cannons or in conjunction with them. Film capacity is 150 exposures; at a speed of 8 frames per second, the S-13 can shoot continuously for 19 seconds.

Crew escape system: The La-15 is equipped with a cartridge-fired ejection seat. The seat pan is dished to take a ribbon-type parachute. Ejection is accomplished by pulling a handle and the canopy is jettisoned automatically in the process. To prevent accidental ejection, two ground safety pins and a flight safety feature are provided.

Chapter 5

Supersonic – At Last

'Aircraft 176' (La-176) Experimental Fighter

When supersonic flight became reality, it was a turning point in world aviation history. As noted earlier, the first attempts to exceed flight speeds around 1,000 km/h (621 mph) revealed a new phenomenon – the aircraft seemed to run into an invisible wall. This was due to the so-called wave crisis, the additional drag of compressed air. This 'sound barrier' made it hard to attain a critical speed lying between 1,100 and 1,200 km/h (683-745 mph), depending on the atmospheric conditions, and accelerate beyond this value to supersonic speeds.

No fundamental theories concerning transonic and supersonic flight existed yet in the late 1940s, forcing aircraft designers and test pilots to work by trial and error in their quest for speed. Back in 1945 the German test pilot Hoffmann working for Messerschmitt AG had reached 920 km/h (571 mph) in a Me 262 Schwalbe twin-turbojet fighter. Yet this proved to be the limit – the machine was unwilling to accelerate even in a shallow dive.

On 7th September 1946 the British pilot Sqn Ldr W. A. Waterton attained 988 km/h (614 mph) in a Gloster Meteor 4 fighter pow-

ered by Rolls-Royce Derwent V turbojets. Not to be outdone, the American pilot Cdr. Turner W. Caldwell set a world speed record by attaining 1,031 km/h (640.663 mph) in the Douglas D-558-I Skystreak straight-wing research aircraft on 20th August 1947.

In the Soviet Union, the first research into transonic speeds was done by TsAGI in the immediate post-war years. Teams of researchers headed by Sergey A. Khristianovich, Gheorgiy P. Svishchev, Yakov I. Serebriyskiy, Vladimir V. Stroominskiy and Gheorgiy S. Büschgens undertook theoreti-

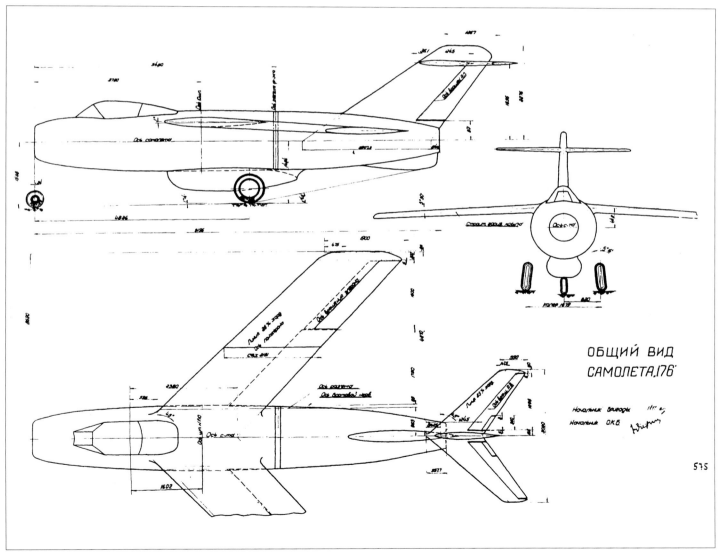

A three-view of the '176' fighter from the project documents, showing the more sharply swept wings.

Above: OKB-301 chief test pilot Ivan Ye. Fyodorov and Chief Designer Semyon A. Lavochkin study western press reports about high-speed flights.

A TsAGI researcher conducts an experiment involving a scale model of the '176' fighter (see opposite page); the needle on the dial may indicate the spatial orientation of the model.

cal and wind tunnel studies of aircraft aerodynamics at transonic speeds, searched for aircraft layouts optimised for such speeds and explored the issues of stability and control in transonic flight.

TsAGI was assisted in this research by LII where flight experiments were undertaken under the guidance of Professor Ivan V. Ostoslavskiy. The so-called 'flying bombs' (LB – *letayushchaya bomba*) – actually gliding models released by an aircraft at high altitude in the manner of bombs to attain transonic speeds in free fall – served to explore the properties of unswept, swept-back, rhomboid and delta wings in these flight modes. Later, the LB models were fitted with solid-fuel rocket boosters ignited after release by the 'mother ship', which allowed them to accelerate beyond Mach 1 in a dive. At the request of LII the Soviet aircraft designer Pavel V. Tsybin developed the Ts-1 rocket-powered research aircraft with interchangeable wing sets which was used in LL-1, LL-2 and LL-3 configurations (unswept, swept-back and forward-swept wings respectively) in 1947-48 to study the transonic airflow over swept wings, record the shock waves and stall areas aft of them as they travelled across the wings, and measure the aerodynamic forces arising in the process. Flight tests with the MiG-15 and La-15 at transonic speeds undertaken by LII yielded invaluable results. Meanwhile, TsIAM and the engine makers were busy developing powerful jet engines and afterburners for them.

The test results obtained with the '160', '174' and '168' fighters reinforced Chief Designer Semyon A. Lavochkin's belief in swept wings and prompted him to take an even more daring step. Based on the successful '168' fighter, a new development aircraft designated '176' was brought out by OKB-301 with the purpose of attaining higher speeds.

The design work commenced in December 1947. The existing fuselage was mated with new wings swept back 45° at quarter-chord and a new, more sharply swept tail unit; the wings had three boundary layer fences each. The powerplant and systems remained unchanged, although there were plans to replace the Rolls-Royce Nene engine with its uprated Soviet derivative, the 2,700-kgp (5,950-lbst) Klimov VK-1, which had just entered production.

Thanks to the considerable commonality with the '168' the prototype was built fairly quickly and rolled out in September 1948. On 22nd September the '176' made its maiden flight at Zhukovskiy with OKB-301 chief test pilot Ivan Ye. Fyodorov at the controls. According to Fyodorov, the aircraft could match the performance of the MiG-15; it was stable and easy to fly, well armed and 500 kg (1,100 lb) lighter than the MiG.

The second flight was made by a young Lavochkin OKB test pilot, Capt. Oleg V. Sokolovskiy. After four more flights from Zhukovskiy at the hands of Fyodorov the manufacturer's flight tests continued at Saki on the Crimea Peninsula, the Ukraine; there, piloted by Sokolovskiy, the '176' made several flights in a stiff crosswind from the Black Sea in late December. Also at Saki, an attempt was made to go supersonic. Due to the insufficient power of the Nene I engine the pilot resorted to the same technique as used with the '160' – the maximum speed was attained in a shallow dive.

One of the attempts ended in success. On 26th December 1948 the '176' and Oleg V. Sokolovskiy gained the distinction of being the first Soviet aircraft and the first Soviet pilot to attain Mach 1, breaking the sound barrier at 9,060 m (29,720 ft). Six such flights were made in December 1948 and January 1949.

Other OKB-301 personnel involved in the tests included project test engineer N. Ya. Heifitz (head of the OKB's aerodynamics section), test engineer R. A. Aref'yev (head of the flight research section), flight opera-

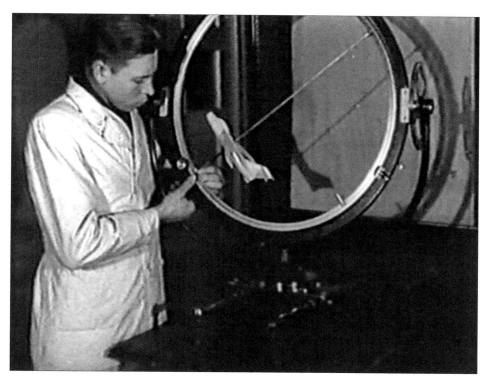

Above and below: Construction of the '176' was preceded by numerous tests involving scale models. Here one such model is mounted on a special test rig with a revolving hoop for manoeuvre simulation.

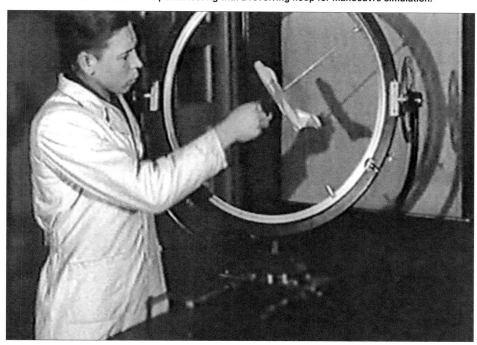

tions engineer V. P. Fridshtand and technician V. S. Alyoshin. A brief report on the attainment of the speed of sound by 'aircraft 176' was completed in the course of the tests; Chief Designer Semyon A. Lavochkin endorsed this document on 29th January 1949. The greater part of the report was concerned not with analysis of the test results but rather with the technique of measuring the speed in transonic flight and the specifications of the instruments used for this. This was indeed important because rock-solid proof

that the aircraft had indeed reached and exceeded the speed of sound had to be presented, considering the numerous sceptics both in the competing OKBs and in the government who would call the achievement into question. Fact is, the very first high-speed dives had indicated that the '176' was capable of going supersonic. The readouts of the test equipment recording the flight parameters showed that the aircraft had passed Mach 1. Yet, doubting the accuracy of the instrument readings, the members of the test

Above and below: The 'aircraft 176' experimental fighter seen during manufacturer's flight tests. While the 45° wing sweep is not apparent here, the photos show clearly the three boundary layer fences on each wing instead of the usual two. Note the rectangular windshield similar to that of the '174D' as first flown.

Above and below: Two more views of the '176'; the lower picture shows that the airbrakes are located further forward than on the La-15. Note the forked pitot on the starboard wing and the additional pitot on the tail.

Above: Front view of the '176'. Note how the black anti-soot panel near the starboard cannon muzzle extends across the nose gear door. The diamond pattern of the mainwheel tyre tread is also noteworthy.

This photo illustrates the strong sweepback of the wings and stabilisers clearly, as well as the triple wing fences.

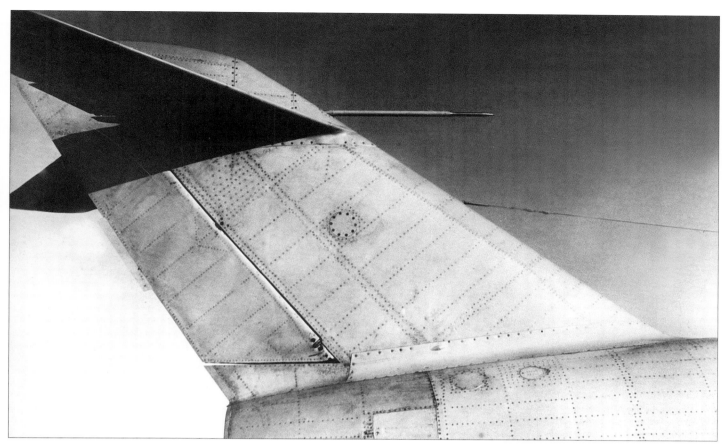

Above: The tail unit of the '176' with the fin-mounted pitot.

The forked wing-mounted pitot. The pitot tubes were specially calibrated in TsAGI's supersonic wind tunnel to make sure the speed measurements would be accurate and dispel any doubts about the speed of sound being achieved.

Above: A preserved Klimov VK-1 turbojet. Such an engine was fitted to the '176' for the series of test flights in which the aircraft reached the speed of sound.

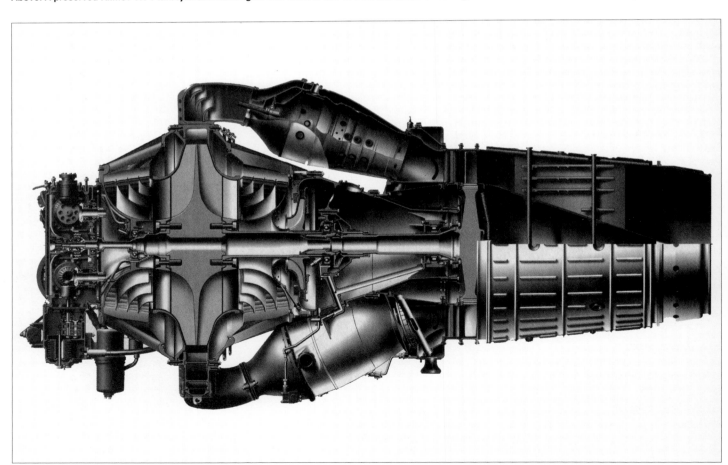

A cutaway drawing of the VK-1.

commission decided to play safe and dispatched project test engineer Heifitz to Moscow with the purpose of calibrating the special supersonic pitot tube in the TsAGI wind tunnel. Once this had been done, a new series of high-speed dives was made and, as mentioned above, on 26th December 1948 Sokolovskiy reached 1,105 km/h (686 mph) while diving from 10,000 m (32,810 ft) to 6,000 m (19,685 ft); this equalled Mach 1.02, or 2% above the speed of sound.

In January 1949 the aircraft was refitted with a VK-1 engine and the tests continued with the objective of reaching the speed of sound. In late January the fighter attained Mach 1.016 in a dive and Mach 0.99 in level flight at 7,500 m (24,610 ft), which equalled a true airspeed of 1,105 km/h. Thus the '176' had considerably higher performance than the Lavochkin OKB's previous aircraft with more moderate wing sweep.

The final part of the report (traditionally called 'Conclusions') read as follows:

'1. 'Aircraft 176' powered by a Nene I engine has attained the speed of sound at 9,060 m in a descent.

2. The same aircraft re-equipped with a VK-1 engine exceeded the speed of sound, reaching Mach 1.016-1.03 (in a descent).

3. When flying at the speed of sound, as well as at supersonic speed, 'aircraft 176' displays no abnormalities in stability and handling; the aircraft's behaviour does not differ significantly from its behaviour at subsonic speeds.

The stability and control characteristics at high Mach numbers recorded during the tests shall be dealt with in a special report.

A speed of Mach 0.99 was attained in level flight.'

The report was signed by test pilot Capt. Oleg V. Sokolovskiy, OKB-301 Deputy Chief Designer L. A. Zaks, project test engineer N. Ya. Heifitz and test engineer R. A. Aref'yev.

Unfortunately the test programme was never completed because the prototype was lost. On 3rd February 1949, just as the '176' became airborne on a routine test flight, the canopy, which had not been closed properly, popped open due to airflow suction. Test pilot Oleg V. Sokolovskiy attempted to re-close it and lost track of the airspeed in so doing; while he was struggling with the canopy, the aircraft lost speed, stalled at low altitude and crashed, killing the pilot.

The accident investigation panel appointed after the crash included the leading Soviet aerodynamicists – Professor Ivan V. Ostoslavskiy, Professor V. N. Matveyev and Professor Vladimir V. Stroominskiy. After analysing all of the flight test materials the panel noted in the accident report:

'In the course of the manufacturer's flight tests, On 26th December 1948 'aircraft 176' powered by a VK-1 engine reached the speed of sound for the first time.

[...] The flight test results obtained with the '176' are of exceptional value for our high-speed aviation. During the month that followed, the speed of sound was attained six times.'

Here it is fitting to quote the memoirs of former OKB-301 chief test pilot Ivan Ye. Fyodorov, HSU. The style of the original text is retained as much as possible.

OKB-301 test pilot Oleg V. Sokolovskiy, one of the two pilots who flew the '176'. He had the honour of breaking the sound barrier for the first time in the Soviet Union in this aircraft on 26th December 1948 – and lost his life in the crash of the same aircraft on 3rd February 1949.

'Before the attempt on the sound barrier it was obvious that there were no guarantees of the pilot surviving. Nobody knew what it is like in practice and whether the aircraft structure would stand up to the force of the elements. Yet, we did our best not to think about it.

What happened was this. From high altitude I accelerated my '176'. I could hear a subdued and constant whine that could set your teeth on edge. Picking up speed, the aircraft hurtled earthwards. On the Mach meter dial, the needle crept from three-digit figures into the four-digit range. (sic – Auth.) The aircraft shook as if in a fit of fever. Then, all of a sudden, there was silence! The sound barrier had been passed. Later, analysis of the oscillogrammes (test equipment oscillograph readouts – Auth.) showed that I had exceeded Mach 1. Oleg Sokolovskiy had obtained similar results. Yet, the overly diligent members of the [test] commission doubted this success, referring to the imperfect inertia-type instruments that could not capture the rapidly developing processes.

Then, engineer Heifitz was dispatched to Moscow and came back to Saki with a special supersonic pitot tube that had been tested at TsAGI. Luckily for us, it turned out that, as distinct from the original pitot (which gave exaggerated speed readings), the new pitot gave understated (albeit slightly) speed readings. We were happy as could be! We were all smiling at each other. Even Semyon Alekseyevich [Lavochkin], a modest person who always looked worried, rejoiced like a kid; he was merry and excited.

Basic Specifications of the 'Aircraft 176'

Powerplant	1 x VK-1
Thrust, kgp (lbst)	2,700 (5,950)
Length overall	10.975 m (36 ft 0 in)
Fuselage length	9.195 m (30 ft 2 in)
Wing span	8.59 m (28 ft 2³⁄₁₆ in)
Stabiliser span	3.0 m (9 ft 10⁷⁄₆₄ in)
Wing area, m² (sq ft)	18.25 (196.23)
Wing sweep at quarter-chord	45°
Empty weight, kg (lb)	3,111 (6,858)
All-up weight, kg (lb):	
estimated	4,631 (10,209) *
actual	4,470 (9,850)
Maximum Mach number attained	1.016-1.03
Maximum speed in level flight at 5,000 m (16,400 ft), km/h (mph)	1,105 (686)
Climb time to 5,000 m, minutes	1.8
Service ceiling, m (ft)	15,000 (49,210)
Estimated range, km (miles)	1,400 (869)
Armament	1 x 37-mm cannon
	2 x 23-mm cannons

* some sources say 4,637 kg (10,222 lb)

Yet our joy was cruelly cut short by a fatal crash – Oleg [Sokolovskiy] crashed on his fourth flight in the La-176 (sic – Auth.). Some publications tell a lot of bull about this accident. What really happened was this. Before taxying out from the hardstand to the runway Oleg received clearance from the tower and raised his hand, signalling "chocks away" to the technician. The technician complied and then, noticing that the canopy locking handle was in the open position, started giving hand signals to the pilot to draw his attention. The pilot gave a gesture of annoyance, showing that he knew about it. However, at the line-up point Sokolovskiy became so engrossed in radio communication with the ATC shift supervisor and forgot about this "trifle". Receiving clearance to take off, he concentrated on the runway, keeping the aircraft on the centreline. When the machine had accelerated to some 300 km/h [186 mph], the slipstream opened the unsecured canopy, which started swinging open to starboard. We may assume that the pilot grabbed hold of the internal canopy handle with his left hand, trying to keep it shut with all his strength while clutching the stick with his right hand and hauling it back in so doing. Travelling at approximately 400 km/h [248 mph] the aircraft pitched up sharply, losing speed, then fell through, rolled and struck the ground…

I regret to sound so pessimistic as I conclude my reminiscences. All I can say is that among the hundreds of test flights I have made, my flights in the '176' stand out in my memory.'

Thus, Lavochkin's 'aircraft 176' was the world's third turbojet-powered aircraft to exceed the speed of sound, closely following the lead set only a few months earlier by the North American XF-86A Sabre fighter prototype and the de Havilland DH.108 Swallow tailless experimental aircraft. Both of these aircraft had likewise broken the sound barrier in a shallow dive; the XF-86A had gone supersonic in April 1948 and the DH.108 in September 1948.

The crash of the '176' (which by then had made 23 flights, including eleven with the VK-1 engine) not only resulted in an abrupt termination of the test programme; it also accounted for the Soviet government's reserved attitude towards the significant achievement made with this aircraft. It was also undoubtedly a factor in the subsequent decision to discontinue production of the La-15 in Gor'kiy. The '176' programme was not resumed because by then the Mikoyan OKB, which was favoured by the government, had by then launched a similar programme with the MiG-15 fighter.

Nevertheless, the '176' paved the way for large-scale exploration and exploitation of transonic and supersonic speeds in the

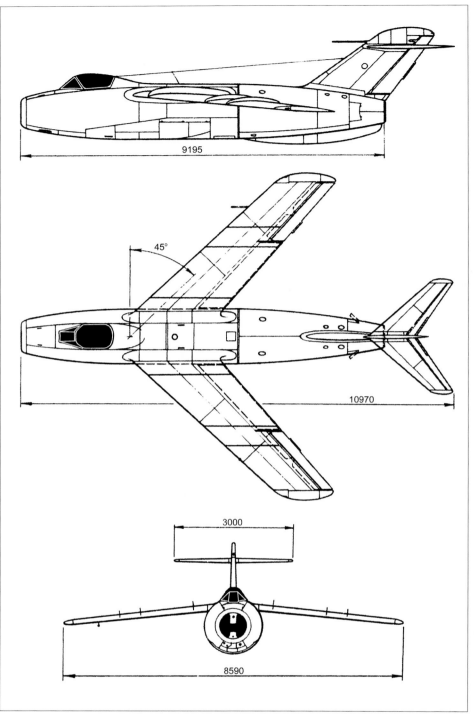

A three-view of the '176' experimental fighter.

Soviet Union. On 18th October 1949 test pilot A. M. Tyuterev attained Mach 1.01 in a shallow dive from 12,800 m (42,000 ft) in the MiG-15LL testbed (*letayushchaya laboratoriya* – lit. 'flying laboratory'; the Russian term for all manner of testbeds and research/survey aircraft). In February 1950 the test pilot Ivan T. Ivashchenko reached 1,114 km/h (691 mph) or Mach 1.03 in level flight in the prototype of the subsequently world-famous MiG-17 (*izdeliye* SI) – a derivative of the MiG-15 (*izdeliye* S) with 45° wing sweep instead of 35°

developed with due regard to the design experience gained with the 'aircraft 176'. Almost concurrently, Yakovlev OKB test pilot Sergey N. Anokhin broke the sound barrier in the Yak-50 development aircraft (the first machine to be thus designated – a single-seat all-weather interceptor). The early experience of transonic flight proved invaluable during the research and development work that culminated in the creation of the MiG-19, the Soviet Union's first production supersonic fighter, in 1953.

Chapter 6

Mismatch

'Aircraft 190' (La-190) Experimental Day Interceptor

In February 1949 the designers of OKB-301 started work on an interceptor that received the in-house designation 'aircraft 190'. In addition to more refined aerodynamics and a higher thrust/weight ratio, the aircraft was characterised by the provision of a *Korshun* (kite, the bird) gun ranging radar and an ASP-3N computing gunsight making it possible to detect and attack the target in adverse weather. The Korshun was a single-antenna radar developed by the NII-17 avionics house under Chief Designer Viktor V. Tikhomirov (now called NIIP – *Naoochno-issledovatel'skiy instit**oot** prib**orostroyen**iya*, Research Institute of Instrument Engineering); it was also fitted to several interceptor prototypes developed by the Mikoyan OKB. This radar lacked automatic target tracking capability, which was a major shortcoming; tracking had to be performed manually, which increased pilot workload.

The aircraft had all-new thin wings swept back 55° at quarter-chord and a high-set horizontal tail of rhomboid planform, which was supposed to facilitate penetration of the 'sound barrier' in level flight. Hence 'aircraft 190' was informally known at the OKB as the *pyatide**syat**ka* ('The Fifty'), the nickname referring to the wing sweep angle. The long and slender fuselage with an unusually high fineness ratio accommodated a powerful Lyul'ka AL-5 axial-flow turbojet; this new engine (also designated TR-3A) delivered 5,000 kgp (11,020 lbst) for take-off.

The control system featured extremely thin and stiff control surfaces and powerful irreversible hydraulic actuators. For the first time in the Lavochkin OKB's practice the aircraft featured a bicycle undercarriage with underwing outrigger struts. The main gear unit had a special 'kneeling' mechanism increasing the landing angle of attack to 20-22°; the purpose of this feature was to reduce the landing speed to a passable 160-170 km/h (99-105 mph). A brake parachute was provided to shorten the landing run. Another 'first' for a Lavochkin aircraft was the use of integral fuel tanks in the wings. The armament consisted of two 37-mm (1.45 cal.) Nudelman N-37 cannons in the lower forward fuselage.

The '190' embodied many innovative and complex features, which led the OKB to build a large number of test rigs for verifying them,

as well as special manufacturing jigs and tooling. Additionally, as recounted in Chapter 3, some of the new interceptor's features (such as the bicycle landing gear) were put through their paces in flight on a specially modified La-15 fighter.

The prototype was competed in February 1951, commencing manufacturer's flight

tests on 21st February with A. G. Kochetkov as project test pilot. Almost immediately the tests were marred by an incident on 6th March when the aircraft suffered damage during a taxi run due to a poorly adjusted engine. The repairs proved rather lengthy and the '190' did not reappear at the flight test facility until 28th May 1951.

The cockpit of the '190' interceptor; the thick bulletproof windshield and the radarscope of the Korshun radar on the right are visible. Note the aircraft silhouette on the left with landing gear position lights.

Above: 'Aircraft 190' was powered by the Lyul'ka AL-5 (TR-3A) axial-flow turbojet. Advanced though it was, the engine proved unreliable and killed off not only the '190' but the Mikoyan I-350 fighter as well.

Above: Another view of the AL-5, showing the jetpipe and the dorsally mounted accessory gearbox.

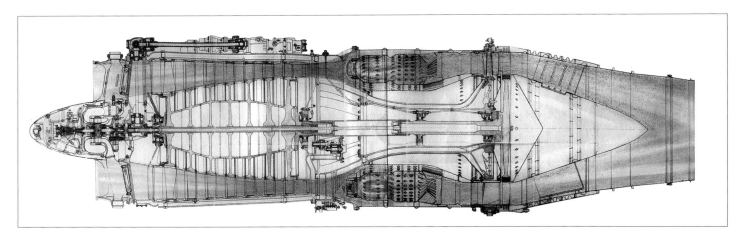

A cross-section of the AL-5 showing the seven-stage compressor, the single-stage turbine and the fixed-area nozzle.

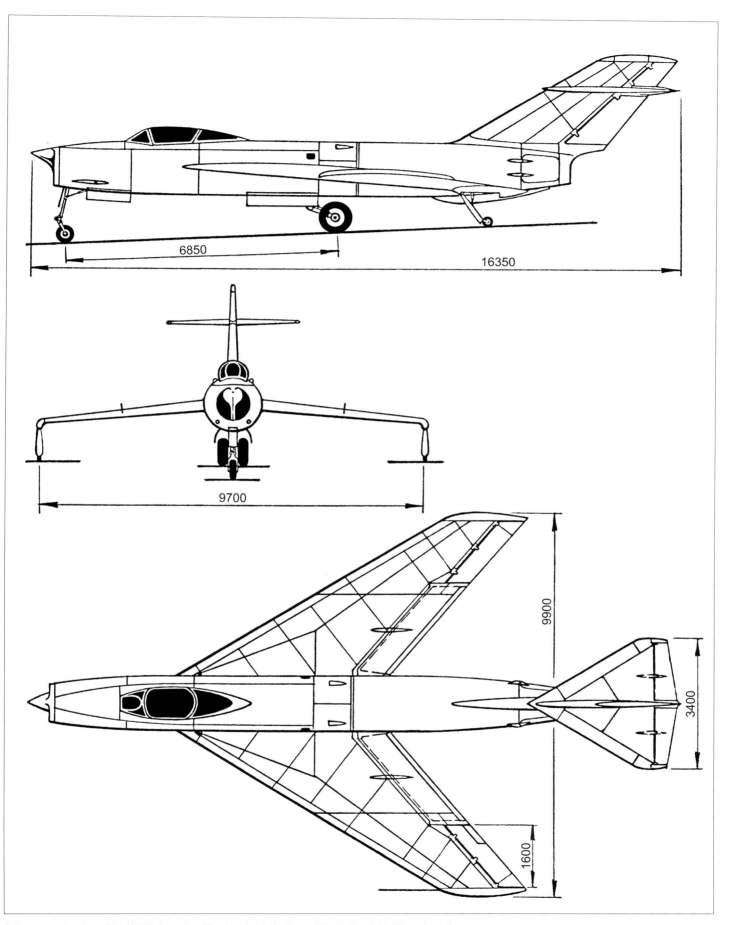

6850

16350

9700

9900

3400

1600

A three-view drawing of the '190' interceptor. The rhomboid planform of the horizontal tail is noteworthy.

Basic Specifications of the 'Aircraft 190' Interceptor

Powerplant	1 x AL-5 (TR-3A)
Thrust, kgp (lbst)	5,000 (11,020)
Length overall	16.35 m (53 ft 7⁴⁵⁄₆₄ in)
Height on ground	4.4 m (14 ft 5¹⁵⁄₆₄ in)
Wing span	9.9 m (32 ft 5¾ in)
Stabiliser span	3.4 m (11 ft 1⁵⁵⁄₆₄ in)
Wing area, m² (sq ft)	38.93 (418.6)
Landing gear track (outriggers)	9.7 m (31 ft 9⁵⁷⁄₆₄ in)
Landing gear wheelbase	6.85 m (22 ft 5¹¹⁄₁₆ in)
Wing sweep at quarter-chord	55°
All-up weight, kg (lb)	9,257 (20,407)
Fuel capacity, litres (Imp gal)	2,100 (462)
Maximum Mach number attained	1.03
Maximum speed in level flight at 5,000 m (16,400 ft), km/h (mph)	1,190 (739)
Climb time to 5,000 m, minutes	1.5
Service ceiling, m (ft)	15,600 (51,180)
Maximum range at 10,000 m (32,810 ft), km (miles)	1,150 (714)
Armament	2 x 37-mm cannons

Above: Before the actual 'aircraft 190' flew, the Lavochkin OKB built a large-scale gliding model that was taken aloft on a special rack by a modified bomber (apparently an Il'yushin IL-28) and released at high altitude.

Despite persistent attempts to adjust the engine in the course of numerous ground runs, the AL-5 kept 'acting up'. In one of the first flights the 'aircraft 190' suffered an engine flameout; luckily the pilot managed to reach the airfield and make a safe landing. On 16th June 1951 the engine flamed out again; this time the outcome was not so good, the aircraft suffering damage in the ensuing crash landing. Despite the Lyul'ka OKB's attempts to cure the AL-5's teething troubles, further flight testing was unsafe, and on 25th August

A cutaway drawing of the '190', showing the 'knee-action' main landing gear strut whose 'kneeling' feature was actuated by a separate hydraulic ram.

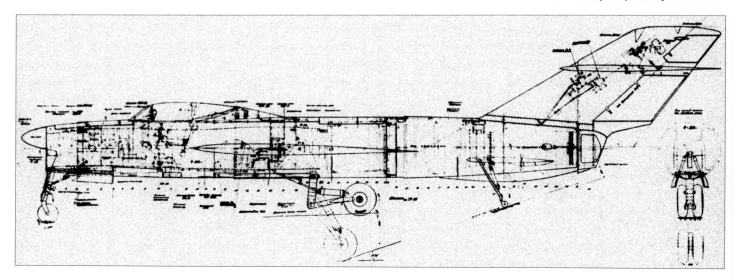

Above and right: A scratchbuilt model of the ill-starred '190' interceptor. These views show to advantage the sharply swept wings and tail surfaces, the flap actuator fairings and the long streamlined cockpit canopy. Note the small auxiliary air scoops on the centre fuselage.

1951 MAP pulled the plug on the programme, ordering a halt.

On the plus side, in the few flights that had been made the '190' demonstrated good performance; the powered controls functioned reliably, and the integral fuel tanks gave no cause for complaint either. Stability and handling at low and medium altitudes were agreeable. At 5,000 m (16,400 ft) the aircraft attained a top speed of 1,190 km/h (739 mph) or Mach 1.03; the service ceiling was 15,600 m (51,180 ft).

Since OKB-301 had higher-priority programmes to take care of and a replacement engine was not available anyway, the flight tests of the '190' never resumed. Thus the partnership between Lavochkin's OKB-301 and Lyul'ka's OKB-165, which appeared to have started out quite well, proved a mismatch after all. It was the same story with the Mikoyan OKB – the I-350 experimental all-weather interceptor (aka *izdeliye* M) designed around the same AL-5 engine fell victim to its incurable tendency to flame out and the programme was terminated after only five flights. On the other hand, the Sukhoi OKB and the Lyul'ka OKB made the perfect pair – a lot of successful Sukhoi aircraft were powered by Lyul'ka engines.

Another view of the same model, showing the small ventral fin.

Above: The only known photo of the '190' interceptor. This view emphasises the long wheelbase and the nose-up ground angle characteristic of aircraft with a bicycle landing gear.

The rival I-350 from the Mikoyan stable was built along more conventional lines but was powered by the same AL-5 engine. The latter's unreliability caused hair-raising incidents with the I-350 as well, and the programme was cancelled after only five flights.

Chapter 7

Gruesome Twosome

'Aircraft 200' (La-200) All-Weather Patrol Interceptor

The rapid development of military technology during the Second World War years brought completely new types of weapons and systems into this world. In the field of aviation, the inventions that shaped the aircraft of the coming years included first and foremost the turbojet engine, airborne intercept (AI) radars used for target detection/rangefinding and aircraft rockets (initially unguided rockets were used against ground and aerial targets alike). After the war, the Soviet government and military high command gave high priority to the development of these technologies, assigning a key role to the aircraft industry. The prototype aircraft construction plan for 1947 drawn up by MAP included jet-powered all-weather interceptors whose development was entrusted to the Mikoyan, Sukhoi and Lavochkin bureaux.

Meanwhile, the aforementioned NII-17 (a specialised avionics design establishment within the MAP framework) embarked on the development of AI radars. By then Soviet spe-

cialists had already amassed some experience in the development of metre-waveband radars, having created the Gneys (Gneiss) AI radar during the war; however, a transition to the centimetre waveband was required in order to improve the radar's detection range and targeting accuracy. The first Soviet centimetre-waveband radar was the *Toriy* (Thorium) radar developed by NII-17 under chief project engineer A. B. Slepushkin. It had a movable parabolic antenna dish and was to be capable of detecting a strategic bomber (such as the Boeing B-29 Superfortress) at up to 12 km (7.45 miles) range.

At first the Sukhoi OKB took the lead in the race of the 'fighter makers'. The Su-15 single-seat interceptor (the first aircraft to bear this designation, aka *izdeliye* P) was rolled out in late 1948. This aircraft with mid-set swept wings and cruciform swept tail surfaces utilised a hitherto unseen powerplant arrangement with two 2,270-kgp (5,000-lbst) Klimov RD-45F centrifugal-flow turbojets, one

Above: A. B. Slepushkin, the designer of the Toriy-A airborne intercept radar developed by NII-17.

The search/tracking antenna, radar set modules and radarscope of the Toriy-A radar prepared for testing.

Above: The single-seat Su-15 of 1948 was the first of the competing twin-turbojet all-weather interceptors utilising the tandem engine placement. The first prototype had a metal fairing instead of the nose radome.

Below: A three-view drawing of the Lavochkin 'aircraft 200' as originally flown; note the drop tanks.

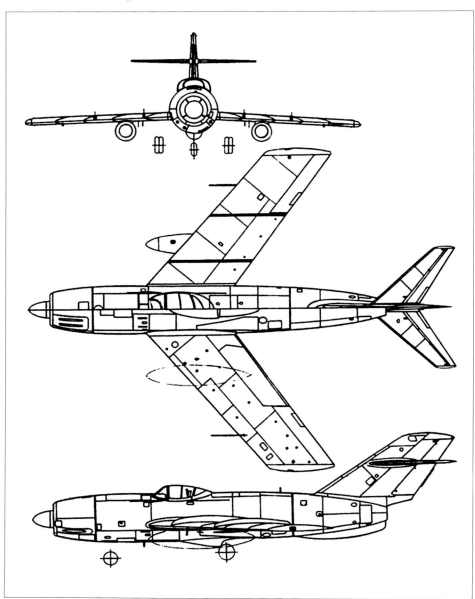

of which was mounted in the nose to exhaust under the centre fuselage via a downward-inclined extension jetpipe and the other was conventionally housed in the rear fuselage. The large semi-elliptical air intake located in the extreme nose was divided by a splitter into two ducts serving the respective engines, with a parabolic radome for the gun ranging radar above it. The armament consisted of two 37-mm (1.45 calibre) Nudelman N-37 cannons buried in the intake's lower lip.

The Su-15 entered flight test on 11th January 1949 and showed excellent performance, but the first prototype crashed on 3rd June that year, breaking up in mid-air at high speed due to wing flutter. This served as a pretext for the closure of the Su-15 programme and the liquidation of OKB-134 as a whole in 1949. After the death of the Soviet leader Iosif V. Stalin and the ensuing liberalisation the Sukhoi OKB was reborn in 1953 as OKB-51 – but that's a different story.

Mikoyan's OKB-155 and Lavochkin's OKB-301 joined in a little later, having various tactical fighter projects to take care of. The Mikoyan OKB's all-weather interceptor designated I-320 (under the pre-war 'by role' designation system that OKB-155 stuck to for a while; I = *istrebitel'* – fighter) and known in-house as *izdeliye* R shared the basic layout of the ill-starred Su-15. So did the Lavochkin contender designated 'aircraft 200' or simply '200'; both aircraft had two turbojets in a staggered-tandem arrangement and armed with heavy cannons. However, unlike the Su-15, both of these aircraft were two-seaters, the crew sitting side by side under a common canopy; the second crewmember was a radar intercept officer (RIO) whose function was to operate the AI radar and provide guidance for the pilot, who concentrated on flying the machine.

During the Great Patriotic War and the immediate post-war years the Lavochkin OKB was among the *crème de la crème* of the Soviet defence industry. The enterprise (both the OKB proper and plant No.301 which hosted it) had considerable design potential and a wealth of experience gained in developing and implementing top-level know-how, supported by its research and development team, test (laboratory) and manufacturing facilities. Therefore, the choice of the Lavochkin design bureau to tackle tasks of prime importance for the defence of the Soviet Union was no matter of chance.

The competing I-320 powered by two RD-45F turbojets and armed with three N-37 cannons had a head start, making its maiden flight on 16th April 1949. At a glance, it seemed that the Lavochkin OKB was dragging its feet. At first the designers of OKB-301 had trouble choosing the right engine for the 'aircraft 200'. The original idea of using two

Above: The competing Mikoyan I-320 (*izdeliye* R) interceptor with its characteristic radome on top of the air intake, which was divided into three channels, and wing-mounted main gear units. The design of the canopy enclosing the side-by-side two-seat cockpit makes the I-320 appear to be grinning evilly.

The 'aircraft 200' as originally built. Note the forward engine jetpipe fairing under the centre fuselage and the small twin mainwheels. The darker forward fuselage with the radome in the middle of the annular air intake was detachable for access to the forward engine.

Above: Front view of the '200' during manufacturer's flight tests. The narrow track of the fuselage-mounted main gear units characteristic of Lavochkin jets is clearly visible, as is the single large bulletproof windscreen. The cannons are installed asymmetrically (one to port and two to starboard).

This side view shows the rear fuselage break point aft of the dorsal IFF aerial and the wide nosewheel well (due to the fact that the nosewheel turned to lie flat during retraction, saving space). Note the drop tanks under the wings.

Above: The '200', still in its original guise with twin mainwheels, is seen here during the first round of state acceptance trials in 1950. Note the four radial struts attaching the intake centrebody 'bullet' housing the radar to the forward fuselage's outer ring.

Another shot of the '200' during state acceptance trials in 1950. The small mainwheels made the fighter look inordinately bulky and heavy.

Above: The '200' is shown here at the Lavochkin OKB's prototype construction facility. Like many Lavochkin prototypes, it wore no insignia whatever. Note the large main gear doors.

The cockpit of the '200' seen during the early stage of the manufacturer's flight tests, showing the dual controls and the absence of some instruments, including the radarscope.

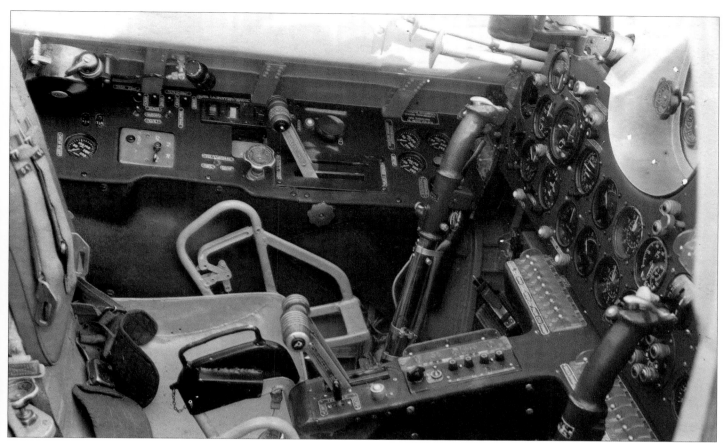

Above: The pilot's (captain's) seat of the '200' and the pilot's control console carrying the throttles. Note the ground safety cover on the ejection seat's actuating handle.

The seat of the radar intercept officer (RIO)/navigator and his side console with controls for the radio and ancillary systems. Note the banks of guarded switches in front of both crewmembers.

Above: This shot with a special superimposed grid was used to assess the field of view from the captain's seat. Note the changes to the instrument panel.

1,590-kgp (3,500-lbst) RR Derwent Vs (Klimov RD-500s) was quickly rejected because the aircraft would be clearly underpowered. This narrowed the choice to two RD-45Fs providing a total of 4,540 kgp (10,000 lbst) or one 4,500-kgp (9,920-lbst) Lyul'ka TR-3 (AL-3) axial-flow turbojet, and the former option was selected eventually. As mentioned earlier, the engines were located in tandem; as distinct from the Su-15, the nose air intake was annular with a bullet-shaped centrebody incorporating the radome. (In contrast, the I-320 had a circular intake divided into three portions by splayed splitters, with the radome on top; the forward engine breathed through the centre portion while the other two portions served the rear engine.) Unlike the Sukhoi and Mikoyan interceptors, 'aircraft 200' had a cigar-shaped fuselage, lacking the other two machines' pronounced 'tadpole effect'; the nozzle of the forward engine was semi-

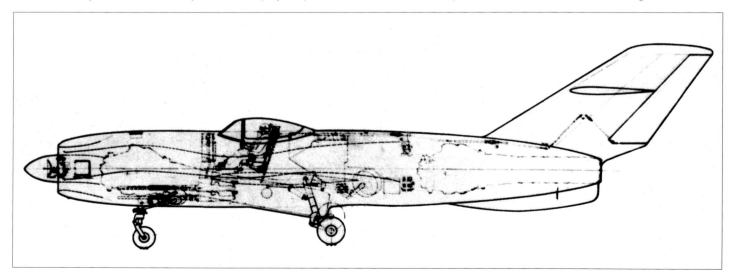

This cutaway drawing shows how the interceptor's inlet ducts were routed and how the aft-retracting landing gear was stowed.

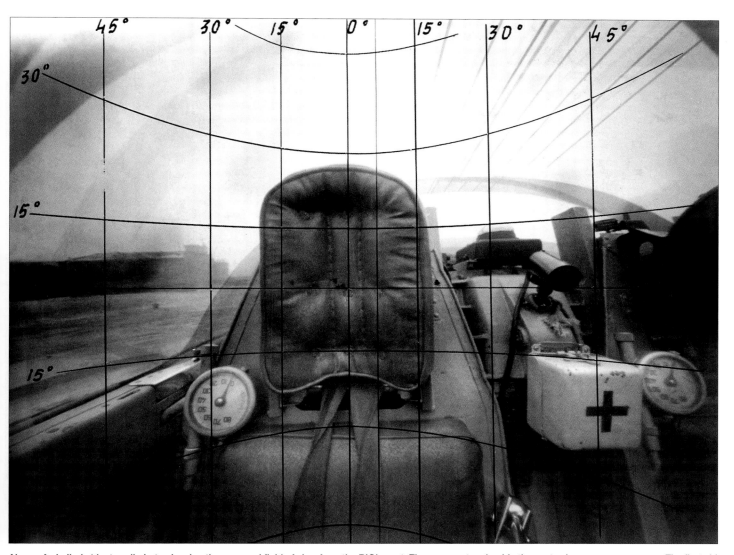

Above: A similarly 'doctored' photo showing the rearward field of view from the RIO's seat. The manometers beside the seats show oxygen pressure. The first aid kit is a particularly neat feature; you don't often see it in a fighter, do you?

recessed in the fuselage, the lower half of the extension jetpipe being enclosed by a small neat fairing.

Another major difference lay in the landing gear design. Unlike the Su-15 and the I-320, which had wing-mounted main gear units retracting inwards so that the single mainwheels stowed in the wing roots, the '200' had aft-retracting fuselage-mounted main gear units. These had levered suspension and were fitted with twin wheels outboard of the oleos to increase the wheel track and reduce the runway loading; the oleos were canted outwards. This made for aerodynamically 'clean' wings whose structural integrity was not compromised by mainwheel wells. The fuselage break point was located aft of the mainwheel wells.

In order to maximise the interceptor's speed performance the designers of OKB-301 opted for wings swept back 40° at quarter-chord and a fairly high wing loading, which was 240 kg/m² (49.2 lb/sq ft) instead of the 200 kg/m² (41.0 lb/sq ft) stipulated by the

Air Force. Hence the RD-45F engines envisaged by the initial project were replaced by an uprated version of the same engine – the Klimov VK-1 non-afterburning turbojet delivering 2,700 kgp (5,950 lbst) for take-off; thus the total available thrust was increased to 5,400 kgp (11,900 lbst). The wings had constant chord and were fitted with two boundary layer fences on each side.

The mock-up review commission examined and approved the full-size mock-up of 'aircraft 200' on 24th February 1949; construction of the first prototype began shortly afterwards. Unlike the single-seat tactical fighters previously created by OKB-301, the interceptor featured a comprehensive mission avionics suite, which included:

• a Toriy-A AI radar;

• an identification friend-or-foe (IFF) system comprising a Magniy-M (Magnesium) interrogator and a Bariy-M (Barium) transponder;

• an ARK-5 Amur automatic direction finder (*avtomaticheskiy rahdiokompas*; Amur,

pronounced like the French word *amour*, is a river in the Russian Far East);

• an RV-2 *Kristall* (Crystal) low-range radio altimeter (*rahdiovysotomer*);

• an MRP-48 *Materik* (Continent) instrument landing system featuring a localiser receiver, a glideslope beacon receiver, a marker beacon receiver and distance measuring equipment. The ILS permitted safe navigation in poor weather and at night; when used jointly with the radar it enabled concerted actions by groups of aircraft.

Other design features worth mentioning included hot-air de-icers on the wing, tail unit and air intake leading edges using engine bleed air. The aircraft's large size and weight required that the '200' be equipped with powered flight controls and high-capacity hydraulic and pneumatic systems. The comprehensive avionics suite also necessitated the provision of a much more powerful electric system than hitherto; also, the primary DC circuit had to be augmented with a high-voltage AC circuit catering for the radar.

Cutaway Drawing Key

1. Movable antenna dish of the Toriy-A radar
2. Radar set
3. Forward VK-1 engine
4. ADF loop aerial
5. ARK-5 Amur ADF
6. MRP-48 Materik ILS modules
7. Ammunition boxes
8. Radarscope
9. PKI back-up optical gunsight
10. Ejection seats
11. Sliding canopy actuating hydraulic ram
12. Forward fuel tank
13. Rear fuel tank
14. Service tank
15. Bariy-M IFF transponder and Magniy-M IFF interrogator
16. IFF interrogator blade aerial
17. Rear VK-1 engine
18. Hot air de-icing system duct
19. Elevator hydraulic actuator
20. RSIU-3 Klyon communications radio antenna
21. ILS antenna
22. Airbrake actuating ram
23. Hydraulic tank
24. RSIU-3 radio set
25. 12A30 DC battery
26. Main landing gear unit

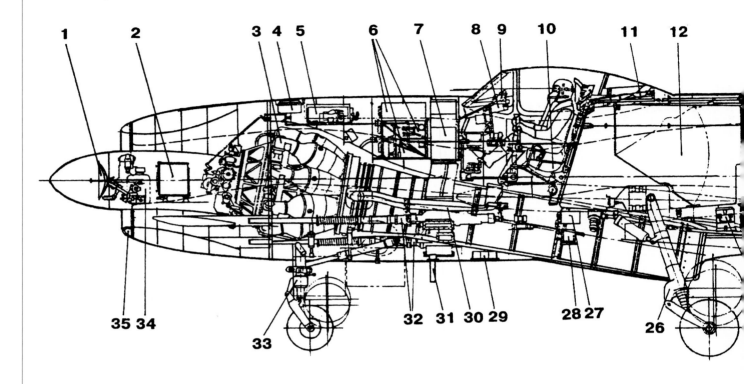

When the prototype had been completed a number of manufacturing defects came to light; yet, even when these had been eliminated, the Lavochkin OKB was in no hurry to roll the aircraft out and commence flight tests. For the first time in the OKB's practice the 'aircraft 200' programme included extensive ground tests of nearly all of the machine's systems and equipment items in simulated operational conditions. This approach was dictated first and foremost by the fact that the designers were venturing into the unknown – never before had OKB-301 designed such a large and heavy aircraft incorporating such a multitude of new and complex equipment. This 'play-it-safe' approach turned out to be a wise one: the ground tests turned up quite a few serious design flaws and manufacturing defects that would have been impossible to rectify in the course of flight tests without incurring major delays.

The manufacturer's flight tests of the '200' officially commenced on 9th September 1949. By then the first prototype of the rival I-320 (designated R-1 – that is, *izdeliye* R No.1)

had been flying for nearly five months – an impressive head start, it would seem. However, by trying to get ahead of the competitor by all means the Mikoyan OKB did itself a disservice. The R-1 turned out to be suffering from a rash of teething troubles; all attempts to cure them were in vain, and in November 1949 the manufacturer's flight tests were abandoned. The first prototype was transferred to NII-17, which used it as an avionics testbed for perfecting the Toriy-A radar. Meanwhile, OKB-155 concentrated on the second prototype I-320 – the R-2, which had VK-1 engines instead of RD-45Fs, a redesigned cockpit canopy offering better visibility and a de-icing system – a feature which the R-1 lacked. The R-2 first flew in the second half of December 1949.

However, Chief Designer Artyom I. Mikoyan was a judicious man who hedged his bets. Thus, in case the I-320 turned out to be a flop, the Mikoyan OKB developed the *izdeliye* SP single-seat all-weather interceptor prototype as an insurance policy. This was a production MiG-15 tactical fighter fitted with

the same Toriy-A radar on the air intake's upper lip; due to the weight of the radar the armament was limited to a single N-37 cannon. A fully functional radar was fitted to the SP in late November 1949 and the Mikoyan OKB embarked on a test programme with the purpose of checking out the radar before submitting the fighter for state acceptance trials. Yet, the single-seat SP did not meet the demands of the military in full.

On 16th September 1949 the first prototype 'aircraft 200' finally made its long-awaited first flight. At the manufacturer's flight test stage the aircraft was flown by OKB-301 test pilots S. F. Mashkovskiy and A. F. Kosarev. Initially the aircraft's all-up weight was limited to 9,910 kg (21,850 lb) because the radar was substituted by ballast. During the initial flight tests the '200' showed excellent speed and rate of climb, reaching 5,000 m (16,400 ft) in 2.35 minutes and 10,000 m (32,810 ft) in 5.85 minutes; the service ceiling was 15,200 m (49,870 ft) and the top speed 1,090 km/h (677 mph) at 3,500 m (11,480 ft). On the other hand, the intercep-

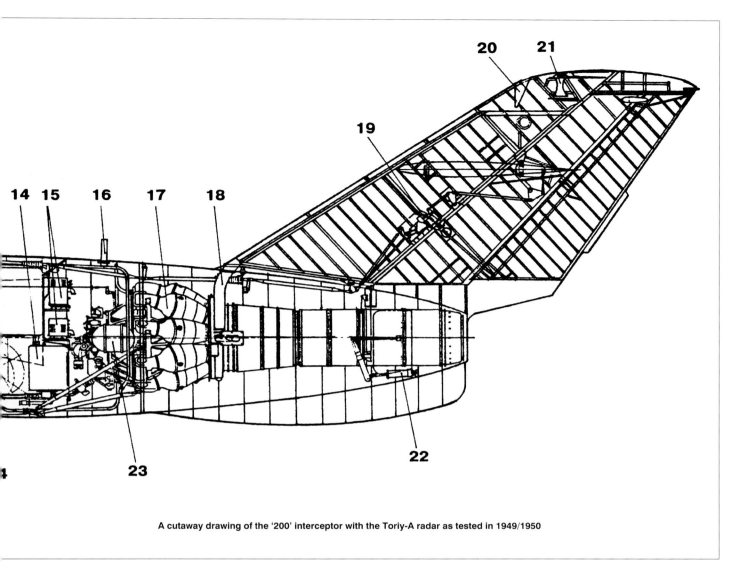

14 15   16   17   18

19

20   21

22

23

A cutaway drawing of the '200' interceptor with the Toriy-A radar as tested in 1949/1950

tor's stability and handling left something to be desired: the stick and pedal forces were excessively high and the aircraft had a tendency to drop a wing at high speeds, rolling to starboard – the tell-tale *val'ozhka* problem.

On 1st December 1949 the aircraft was returned to the Lavochkin OKB's prototype construction facility for modifications. As an anti-*val'ozhka* measure the ailerons were provided with trim tabs making it possible to balance the aircraft at any speed. Later, however, the incidence of the starboard wing was increased by 1°30'; that took care of the problem. The hydraulic actuators in the control system were revised and the missing radar was installed. This increased the AUW to 10,205 kg (22,500 lb), which would inevitably have an adverse effect on the aircraft's performance.

On 13th January 1950 the modified 'aircraft 200' returned to the flight test facility in Zhukovskiy. The very first post-modification flights showed that nearly all of the problems had been addressed; no *val'ozhka* was experienced any more.

The Toriy-A radar and other avionics were checked out in flight in early February. Some of the radar trials sorties were flown solo, while others involved a Lisunov Li-2 transport (a Soviet-built Douglas DC-3 derivative) used as a practice target; six intercepts of the Li-2 were made at up to 7 km (4.34 miles) range. The crew rated the presentation of the target on the radarscope as good. The manufacturer's flight tests were completed on 10th February, whereupon it was decided to submit the interceptor for state acceptance trials; by then the '200' had logged a total of 18 hours 33 minutes in 40 flights.

Yet, turning the machine over to the Air Force for further testing turned out to be not that easy. GK NII VVS subjected the new two-seat interceptor and its mission equipment to rigorous testing involving a lot of checkout flights; the military were especially wary of the radar. It took a personal letter from Chief Designer Semyon A. Lavochkin to Nikolay A. Bulganin, Vice-Chairman of the Soviet Council of Ministers, who was then responsible for aviation matters in the Soviet government, to

get the machine cleared for state acceptance trials. This took place on 12th April 1950; thus, for once, 'aircraft 200' was ahead of its I-320 competitor.

However, Lavochkin's interceptor was not out of the woods yet. The state acceptance trials got off to a brisk start: between 12th April and 3rd May the aircraft made 31 test flights. At this stage the '200' was flown by GK NII VVS test pilots Ivan M. Dzyuba, V. G. Ivanov and V. P. Trofimov. The trials revealed a few unpleasant phenomena that had not been detected until then. Exploring the limits of the interceptor's flight envelope and trying out the most unconventional flight modes, the military test pilots discovered that vibration of the rear fuselage set in when the rear engine was throttled back to flight idle at indicated airspeeds (IAS) in excess of 650 km/h (403 mph) while the forward engine was running at full power. Furthermore, it turned out that *val'ozhka* had not been eliminated completely after all; the aircraft had a tendency to drop the port wing at indicated airspeeds in excess of 820 km/h (509 mph). The twin mainwheels

Above: This picture taken during Stage A of the state acceptance trials in 1950 shows how the nose section was detached together with the radar and wheeled away on a dolly for access to the forward engine. Note the blast plates around the cannon muzzle openings.

Seen shortly afterwards minus nose fairing/radar and forward engine, the '200' shows off the new large single mainwheels that replaced the unsatisfactory twin units. The rear engine's lateral inlet ducts are clearly visible. Note the addition of Soviet Air Force insignia.

Above: Here the aircraft is shown undergoing state acceptance trials after the first round of modifications. The new single mainwheels have required bulges to be made on the mainwheel well doors.

The modified interceptor with drop tanks attached. The faired attachment struts are clearly visible. In a departure from the then-current standard, the national insignia are not applied to the rear fuselage, being carried on the wings and tail only (as became customary after 1954).

Above: The components of the new Korshun radar developed by NII-17 and fitted to the '200' in 1951. The radarscope is quite compact, as is the antenna dish.

Left: A three-view of the '200' in its 1951 configuration with the Korshun radar. The drop tanks are depicted inaccurately (see the photo on the opposite page).

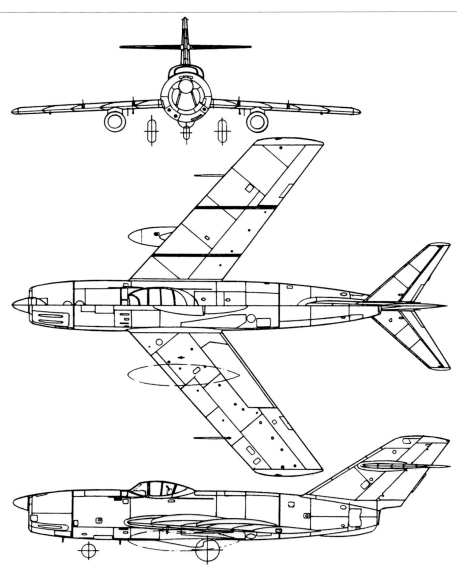

turned out to be troublesome, failing every now and then, and the RSIU-3 radio functioned unreliably. On 3rd May the military got fed up with this and suspended the trials, returning the aircraft to the Lavochkin OKB so that the defects could be rectified.

Here it should be noted that shortly before the '200' commenced trials at GK NII VVS, the Mikoyan OKB had submitted the single-seat SP for state acceptance trials, while the Toriy-A radar common to these aircraft had begun state acceptance trials in the first prototype I-320. The trials of the radar were managed by a State commission chaired by Lt. Gen. Yevgeniy Ya. Savitskiy, Commander of the National Air Defence Force's fighter arm (IA PVO – *Istrebitel'naya aviahtsiya* **Protivovozdooshn**oy **oboron**y). The first results of the radar's trials gave little reason to rejoice; the Toriy-A was rather troublesome and beset by development problems. Target detection range in pursuit mode for a heavy bomber such as the Tupolev Tu-4 varied from 3 to 7 km (1.86-4.34 miles) and the radar frequently failed. As for the Mikoyan SP, the commission concluded that using a single-seat fighter equipped with a radar in the interceptor role was extremely complicated – the pilot found it extremely difficult or even downright impossible to fly the aircraft and watch the radarscope at the same time during the attack (the

The GK NII VVS test pilots who flew the '200' interceptor during state acceptance trials. Left to right: S. F. Mashkovskiy, Mark L. Gallai and I. K. Vedernikov.

radarscope had to be monitored continuously while closing in on the target).

Meanwhile, Lavochkin OKB test pilots made a series of 24 test flights, trying to determine the cause of the vibrations affecting the rear fuselage of 'aircraft 200'. It turned out that when the rear engine was throttled back and its mass flow reduced, the air pressure distri-bution pattern on the fuselage changed, creating large low-pressure areas on the forward fuselage. The turbulent boundary layer in these areas became thicker, generating powerful vortices and causing vibration. Moreover, when the rear engine was throttled back the ejector effect of its exhaust jet vanished, further spoiling the airflow around the rear fuselage. The specialists of GK NII VVS came up with an unusual solution: they suggested making a flight or two with the rear engine's maintenance hatches left open. It worked; the air escaping from the rear engine bay changed the airflow pattern around the rear fuselage and the vibration disappeared. Accordingly the rear fuselage was modified to

A retouched photo of the '200' modified to take the Korshun radar in 1951. Note the modified drop tanks set farther apart from the wing undersurface.

Above and below: These views of the modified '200' taken during state acceptance trials give a better idea of the interceptor's first 'nose job' associated with the Korshun radar. Instead of drop tanks the machine is fitted with six launch rails for unguided rockets. Note also the new dielectric fin cap.

Above and below: Front and rear views of the converted '200' – in this case, without the rocket launch rails. The air intake design is quite similar to that of the Mikoyan I-320. Though it would win no prizes at a beauty contest, the '200' was rather more elegant than its Mikoyan competitor.

Above and below: The Korshun-equipped '200' with drop tanks attached sits in the sun on the GK NII VVS hardstand at Chkalovskaya AB. The aircraft is already showing signs of wear and tear resulting from the intensive trials.

The Korshun radar also found use in the Yakovlev Yak-50 experimental single-seat interceptor. Like many Yakovlev combat jets, it featured a bicycle landing gear for the purpose of reducing structural weight.

incorporate special air spill doors that opened automatically when the rear engine was throttled back. Also, the shape of the fin/fuselage fairing was revised and the shield around the rear engine's jetpipe was more carefully sealed.

Trying to pinpoint the cause of the persistent wing drop problem, the engineers fitted 'aircraft 200' with two cine cameras pointing at the wings. The main cause was quickly traced to the starboard flap which opened spontaneously at high speeds due to airflow suction; it turned out that its uplocks had been improperly adjusted. In order to rectify this fault and improve roll control the aircraft was subjected to the following alterations:

• the flaps were stiffened and their uplocks were readjusted;

• bendable trim tabs (called *nozhee* – 'knives' – in Soviet terminology) 35 mm (1⅜ in) wide were riveted to the wing trailing edge inboard of the ailerons and adjusted to counter the wings' aerodynamic asymmetry;

• the wings' torsional stiffness was increased 30% by adding a number of steel and duralumin stringers to the wing structure;

• the aileron control circuit was revised by installing two hydraulic actuators instead of the original single actuator, which was located in the cockpit aft of the seats.

Apart from that, the main landing gear units were fitted with single large brake-equipped wheels replacing the pairs of stock 660 x 160 mm (26.0 x 6.3 in) wheels used hitherto, and the mainwheel well doors were modified accordingly. The new experimental mainwheels measured 900 x 275 mm (35.43 x 10.82 in). Also, the RSIU-3 communications radio, which was housed near the forward engine's jetpipe, was provided with a ram air cooling system to prevent overheating and failure.

Once the most serious deficiencies had been dealt with, Stage B of the state acceptance trials began. Between 29th July and 16th September 1950 'aircraft 200' made a further 57 test flights under this programme. The interceptor showed fairly high performance: the maximum speed of 1,062 km/h (659 mph) attained at 4,500 m (14,760 ft) was higher than the figure specified by the government. On the minus side, range on internal fuel at 10,000 m (32,810 ft) was only 1,025 km (636 miles) instead of the stipulated 1,500 km (931 miles), although the range target of 2,000 km (1,242 miles) with drop tanks was met. Stability and handling were on a par with single-seat fighters of the day.

A major design defect surfaced at this point – the powered controls were incapable of operating under negative-G conditions. On 25th August 1950 the hydraulic actuators went down after the '200' had flown inverted for 15 seconds. As the pilots attempted to roll the aircraft right side up, the interceptor spontaneously flicked into a tight left spiral; it took the combined efforts of both pilots to recover from the spin after throttling back and deploying the airbrakes. In so doing the aircraft attained 1,018 km/h (632 mph) IAS or Mach 0.986, pulling nearly 5Gs in the spin. Vibration was detected at speeds above Mach 0.82 when drop tanks were fitted; furthermore, the cannons were prone to jamming if the aircraft was pulling positive G while firing.

Despite these shortcomings, 'aircraft 200' received a generally positive appraisal from the State commission. The major issue now was the type of radar to be fitted to the interceptor. The Toriy-A radar had failed its state acceptance trials in the Mikoyan I-320 and had functioned unsatisfactorily throughout the trials of the Lavochkin interceptor as well (only three out of 19 test missions associated with the radar had been accomplished). Aware of the radar's dismal performance, NII-17 was already working on new and more capable AI radars – the Korshun (Kite) single-antenna radar, likewise developed under project chief A. B. Slepushkin, and the RP-1

Izumrood-1 radar (Emerald-1; RP = *rahdio-pritsel* – radio sight) with separate search and tracking antennas developed under project chief Viktor V. Tikhomirov. Both of these radars had comparable dimensions to the Toriy radar, which meant they could be fitted quickly to 'aircraft 200'. The Lavochkin OKB picked the Korshun.

Meanwhile, the Mikoyan OKB endeavoured to submit the second prototype I-320 (the R-2) for state acceptance trials; however, this aircraft was found to be suffering from the same defects as the first one. By September 1950 no cure had been found, even though the machine had made 100 flights by then. The deadline was approaching, and on 20th September the R-2 was submitted to GK NII VVS in as-was condition – in what might be called a gesture of despair, since the defects were still there. Small wonder that the state acceptance trials were suspended only ten days later (on 20th September) after 24 flights because the interceptor suffered from lateral instability at Mach 0.89-0.9 and *val'ozhka* at speeds above 840-930 km/h (521-577 mph) IAS.

At this point it is appropriate to digress a little. In the early 1950s, when the West and the Soviet Union alike were actively developing air-launched nuclear weapons and delivery vehicles for same, the KB-1 design bureau established within the framework of the Soviet Ministry of Armament began development of 'unmanned aerial intercept systems' – or, putting it plainly, surface-to-air missiles (SAMs). Unlike cannon-armed interceptors equipped with radars, which were capable of attacking the potential adversary's bombers only from the rear, SAMs guided from the ground could engage an aerial target from any quarters. SAM development in the Soviet Union was triggered by Korean War experience. The US Air Force launched massive formations of heavy bombers and attack aircraft against North Korean targets; although Korean People's Army Air Force fighters claimed their share of 'kills', most of the American aircraft usually managed to press on and inflict great damage. In a nuclear war scenario such a prospect was totally unacceptable for the Soviet government and military leaders.

Furthermore, the limited armament and avionics of the day's all-weather interceptors made it imperative to guide them accurately towards the target by means of ground controlled intercept (GCI) centres if the target was to be destroyed. Mission success depended equally on the pilots' skill and on the skill of the GCI crews. The probability of intercepting and destroying a solitary high-speed target was no more than 60% if the target aircraft just pressed on towards its objective; if the target started making evasive manoeuvres or using electronic countermeasures (ECM), the chances of success were much lower. That said, the idea of using an air defence system based on cannon-armed all-weather interceptors to repel a massive raid by enemy bombers carrying nuclear weapons did not appeal to anyone.

Yet, at that time MAP did not have any better offers. The Soviet aircraft industry was not in a position to develop guided air-to-air missiles for the interceptors on its own because the abovementioned Ministry of Armament had 'staked its claim' to the development of all guidance systems for unmanned aerial vehicles (including missiles) back in the late 1940s.

As a result, in the early 1950s the Soviet political and military leaders lost interest in cannon-armed interceptors. Thus, despite the higher performance of the '200' as compared to the rival I-320, the future of this aircraft was very much in doubt.

Yet the task of creating radar-equipped interceptors was still there – for more than one reason. Firstly, the Ministry of Armament had started work on air-to-air missiles that were to become the intercepts' new weapon; secondly, the radar designers were not sitting idle either and more advanced models were under development. Finally, although missile systems were now strongly on the agenda, the Soviet government chose not to place its bets entirely on SAMs – like any new type of weaponry, they could well give nasty surprises. Thus, development of manned interceptors continued as a 'belt-and-braces' policy.

Hence OKB-301 started adapting the '200' to take the new Korshun radar. This necessitated a redesign of the forward fuselage. The radome was moved to the intake's upper lip and the intake itself was divided into three sections by splayed splitters, as on the I-320; the forward engine breathed through the centre portion while the other two portions served the rear engine. This made it possible to alter the airflow pattern around the rear fuselage and eliminate the famous vibrations without resorting to the air spill doors used on the first prototype.

Other changes included the addition of flight spoilers; these were used to assist the ailerons for roll control, improving high-speed handling. The IFF interrogator and transponder were relocated to the forward fuselage, making it possible to increase the capacity of the rear fuel tank by 250 litres (55 Imp gal); however, this 250-litre appendage to the fuel tank was only a mock-up installation. The drop tanks were reshaped to reduce drag, with longer and more streamlined struts. The defects of the cannon armament noted in the course of the trials were rectified.

After an extensive conversion the '200' prototype commenced a new round of manufacturer's flight tests (involving 114 flights) on 29th January 1951; these were followed by renewed state acceptance trials on 6th March – 13th April. Both test programmes took place at the GK NII VVS facility at Chkalovskaya AB east of Moscow. The state acceptance trials programme included 129 flights; 40% of these were made in adverse weather (heavy cloud with a cloudbase of 150 m (490 ft) and an upper limit of up to 9,500 m (31,170 ft), as well as rain and snow) and a further 12 flights were made at night. Thus by the end of the trials the aircraft had made a total of 243 flights.

The new round of state acceptance trials showed that the modified interceptor's performance was slightly improved on all counts. The aircraft had a maximum speed of 1,070 km/h (664 mph) at 5,000 m (16,400 ft), climbing to 10,000 m (32,810 ft) in six minutes flat; the service ceiling was 15,550 m (51,020 ft). Had the capacity of the rear fuel tank actually been increased by 250 litres, the range would have been 1,170 km (726 miles) on internal fuel only and 2,170 km (1,347 miles) with drop tanks. However, the Korshun radar was non-functional and its performance was not checked at this point, this part of the trials being postponed until summer.

The concluding part of the trials report said, '... 'aircraft 200' has passed the trials with satisfactory results and is recommended for series production. The airframe design allows for the installation of Korshun or Izumrood radars. The choice of the radar [for the production version] shall be made proceeding from the results of the radars' state acceptance trials.'

A while later the I-320 also completed a new round of state acceptance trials. Despite the efforts of the Mikoyan OKB, some of the I-320's deficiencies persisted; moreover, the trials were marred by an incident in the course of live firing tests when a cannon shell exploded immediately after leaving the barrel, inflicting heavy damage to the forward fuselage. The ensuing repairs and modifications caused further delays and the trials were finally completed on 23rd April 1951 – with unsatisfactory results.

Thus, by the spring of 1951 Lavochkin's 'aircraft 200' was the only Soviet two-seat all-weather interceptor – and the only one of the competing tandem-engine designs – to pass state acceptance trials satisfactorily and be cleared for production. On 23rd May 1951 a draft directive ordering the '200' into production under the service designation La-17 was submitted to the Soviet Council of Ministers; the aircraft was to be produced by plant No.21 in Gor'kiy, a long-standing partner of the Lavochkin OKB. MAP was already drafting a revised production plan for the Gor'kiy factory tasking its with manufacturing the first 50 production La-17s by the end of the year. Eventually, however, the CofM directive was never endorsed and production failed to materialise. (As already noted, the designation La-17 was reassigned to a target drone.)

'Aircraft 200B' All-Weather Patrol Interceptor Prototype;
'Aircraft 200BF' All-Weather Patrol Interceptor (project)

It should be noted that the Korshun radar also attracted the attention of OKB-115 headed by Chief Designer Aleksandr S. Yakovlev. The Yak-50 single-seat interceptor powered by a single VK-1 turbojet and fitted with this radar (the first aircraft to bear this designation) passed state acceptance trials in June 1951 with unsatisfactory results. After that, the Yakovlev OKB began development of the Yak-120 two-seat interceptor equipped with a Sokol (Falcon) AI radar – another NII-17 product. This aircraft was intended to operate primarily from airbases in the Soviet High North and Far East – areas where the Soviet military high command considered it inadvisable to field SAM systems. The Sokol radar had a target detection range of some 30 km (18.6 miles); the aircraft was powered by two new Mikulin AM-5 axial-flow non-afterburning turbojets which were more fuel-efficient than existing engines, making for a range of 3,000-3,500 km (1,863-2,174 miles). The Yak-120 eventually entered production and service as the Yak-25.

In August 1951 the Council of Ministers issued new assignments to two of the Soviet 'fighter makers'. The Mikoyan OKB was entrusted with developing a long-range escort fighter powered by two AM-5s, while the Yakovlev OKB was tasked with creating a two-seat fighter designed around the same powerplant in patrol interceptor and photo reconnaissance versions. MAP was quite happy with this assignment, since funds for new programmes would be allocated; conversely, the PVO's fighter arm was losing out, since development and deliveries of new all-weather interceptors were postponed indefinitely. An unhappy Lt Gen Fyodor A. Agal'tsov (the acting Commander-in-Chief of the Soviet Air Force) sent the following memorandum to the Soviet leader Iosif V. Stalin:

'It will take 18 to 24 months for the new Mikulin-engined aircraft whose development has been assigned to the designers Comrade Mikoyan and Comrade Yakovlev to be put into production and fielded by the Air Force. Until then, I request that the possibility of launching production of a two-seat interceptor designed by Comrade Lavochkin and, if necessary, using it operationally for intercepting hostile aircraft be considered.'

IA PVO Commander Yevgeniy Ya. Savitskiy, too, wrote a memo – this time to CofM Vice-Chairman Nikolay A. Bulganin:

'...I hereby request you to consider the possibility of launching production of the '200' two-seat interceptor developed by Comrade Lavochkin and equipped with a Korshun or Izumrood target detection/aiming radar.'

Being the cautious person he was, Bulganin could not question the rightness of the decisions taken at the top level. Therefore he suggested a compromise solution to MAP – the IA PVO would receive the '200' as an interim type until the new Yak-120 two-seater became available. By fitting the Sokol radar to the fairly successful 'aircraft 200' MAP hoped to kill three birds with one stone, so to say. Firstly, the radar intended for the Yak-120 could be verified; secondly, aircrews would receive initial conversion training on the Lavochkin interceptor, which would facilitate the subsequent transition to the Yakovlev type; finally, the IA PVO would receive the all-weather interceptor it needed.

By then OKB-301 had switched to designing rockets and missiles; moreover, Chief Designer Semyon A. Lavochkin had taken an interest in this new field and was not too happy with the prospect of having to deal with 'aircraft 200' again. Yet, some members of the OKB's design staff insisted on trying to adapt the interceptor to the new requirements and eventually got their way. After all, the aircraft had reached a fairly high degree of refinement and, given a successful upgrade, it might well compete with Yakovlev's 'paper interceptor'. Hence the programme was dusted off, and the new assignment was formally endorsed in mid-November 1951.

Here, mention should be made of Gheorgiy N. Babakin, head of OKB-301's newly established control systems and flight simulation department. He was a workaholic and a

Above: Gheorgiy N. Babakin, head of the Lavochkin OKB's control systems and flight simulation department. He was instrumental in the OKB's decision to go ahead with the '200B' interceptor equipped with the Sokol radar.

person totally engrossed in his work; he was one of those who floated the idea of reviving the '200' programme. Babakin played a decisive role in the subsequent testing and verification of the radar and semi-automatic guidance systems on the '200' and '200B'. A unique ground test and research facility created at OKB-301 under his direction boosted the importance of ground tests of a new aircraft's systems before they were installed in the actual airframe. Semyon A. Lavochkin's

The antenna array and radar set of the Sokol radar developed for the Yak-120 (Yak-25) interceptor.

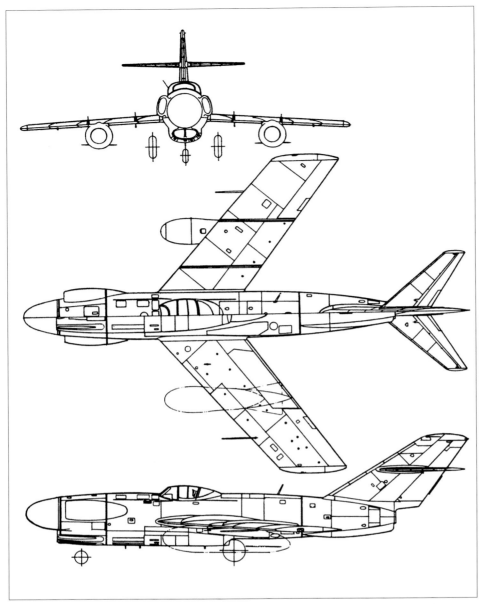

Above: A three-view of the redesigned '200B' interceptor equipped with the Sokol radar. Note the twin ventral fins and the new large conformal drop tanks.

former aide (Deputy Chief Designer) Professor N. S. Chernyakov, who later joined the Sukhoi OKB and headed the development of the famous T-4 supersonic reconnaissance/strike aircraft, describes Babakin's work well in his memoirs:

'...Gheorgiy Nikolayevich Babakin [...] joined the OKB at exactly the right time, and he was the right person for the job. He was a well-educated man and his deep knowledge of radio equipment, electronics and automatic systems was a key factor behind the success of many of our projects. [...] The advent of radars, semi-automatic control systems (GCI command link systems – Auth.), computers and rocket armament changed the outlook of [combat] aircraft and the methods of their design completely; instead of designing simply an aeroplane (where the work was concerned chiefly with the airframe) we had to create highly complex integrated weapons systems. G. N. Babakin played a major role – in many cases, a decisive role – in this.'

Pursuant to the government directive the 'aircraft 200' interceptor redesigned to take the Sokol radar (this version was designated '200B') was to be submitted for state acceptance trials as early as April 1952. A month after this directive the government followed up with another document stipulating that the '200B' was to be armed with three types of unguided rockets – two 212-mm (8.35-in) ARS-212 high-velocity aircraft rockets (HVARs) on APU-O-212 launchers, or four 190-mm (7.48-in) TRS-190 HVARs in paired ORO-190 launch tubes, or sixteen 57-mm (2.24-in.) ARS-57 folding-fin aircraft rockets (FFARs) in two launch pods. (ARS = *aviatsionnyy reaktivnyy snaryad* – [rocket (HVAR). ORO-190 = *odinochnoye reaktivnoye oroodiye [dlya snaryadov kalibra] 190 millimetrov* – launch tube, single, for 190-mm HVARs; APU-O-212 = *aviatsionnaya pooskovaya oostanovka, odinochnaya, [dlya snaryadov*

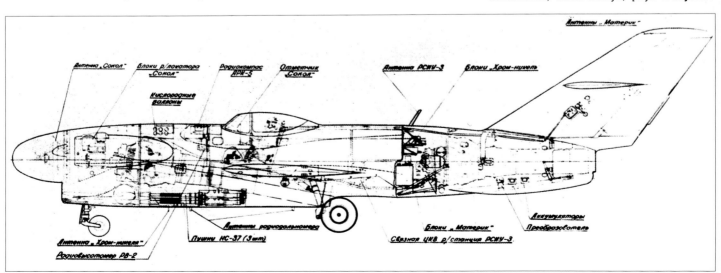

A cutaway drawing of the '200B' showing the upward-curving inlet duct of the forward engine and the revised nose gear unit (the nosewheel stows vertically).

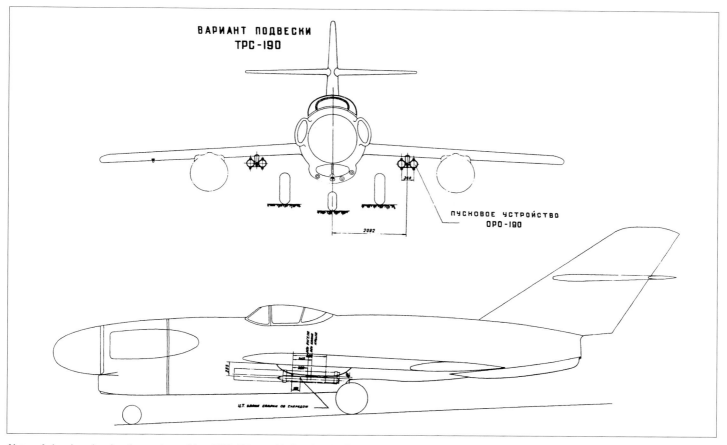

Above: A drawing showing the carriage of four TRS-190 unguided rockets in ORO-190 paired launch tubes on the inboard hardpoints of the '200B'.

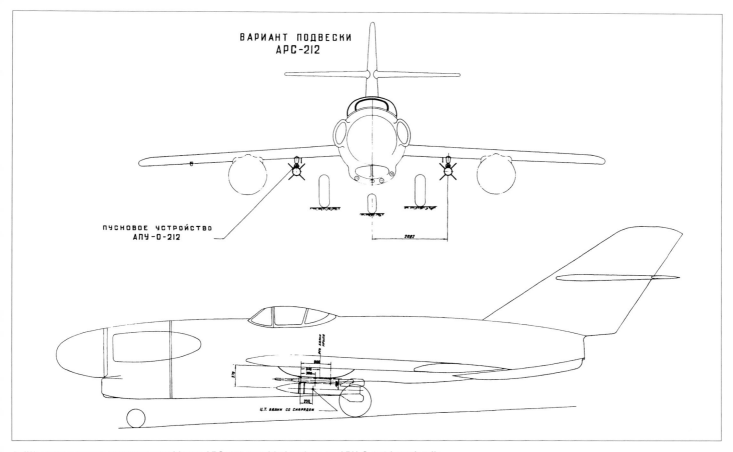

A different armament arrangement with two ARS-212 unguided rockets on APU-O-212 launch rails.

Above: Front view of the radically reworked '200B'. The three air intakes arranged around the huge 'dog nose' radome of the Sokol radar made the fighter look really hideous.

This side view shows clearly the longer landing gear wheelbase of the '200B'. Interestingly, the cannon arrangement was reversed on this aircraft (two to port and one to starboard). Note also the short splayed ventral fins and the new rod aerial of the RSIU-3 radio on the rear fuselage.

Above and below: Here the '200B' is shown with the huge 2,350-litre (583 Imp gal) slipper tanks developed for it. Note the stabilising fins low on the rear portions of the tanks.

Another aspect of the '200B' with drop tanks in place.

kalibra] 212 millimetrov – aircraft-mounted launcher, single, for 212-mm HVARs; also called PU-21.) The reasoning behind this was that the work on guided air-to-air missiles was progressing slower than anticipated, and heavy bombers were hard to destroy with cannon fire alone. Heavy rockets – even unguided ones – would inflict much greater damage, improving 'kill' probability dramatically; a direct hit by even a single HVAR left the bomber no chances of survival. The second directive required the rocket-armed version of the '200B' to be submitted for checkout trials in September 1952.

The installation of the new radar required a major redesign of the airframe. At that time plant No.301 was heavily burdened with missile programmes and was not in a position to meet the deadline; only a partial rebuild of the existing '200' prototype was possible within the specified time limit. Hence the designers came up with two alternative projects; the partial conversion serving as a 'dogship' for verifying the new systems and associated features was known as the '200B', whereas the 'full option' intended for production and meeting the Air Force's requirements in full was designated '200BF'.

Fitting the Sokol radar was not easy at all. This single-antenna radar had a much larger antenna dish than the Korshun, necessitating a complete redesign of the forward fuselage and significant alterations to the centre fuselage. The nose of the '200B' incorporated a huge parabolic radome with three air intakes arranged around it; the forward engine now breathed through a chin-mounted elliptical air intake with a short curved air duct, while two

smaller 'elephant's ear' air intakes were located on the fuselage sides in line with the ventral intake, serving the rear engine. The new intakes increased the airframe drag a good deal. The nose landing gear unit was moved forward, increasing the wheelbase, and redesigned (the nosewheel no longer needed to lie flat under the forward engine when retracted). Changes were made to the cockpit area, and the single ventral fin gave place to two shorter splayed fins.

Apart from the radar, the avionics suite of the '200B' included an ARK-5 ADF, an SP-50 Materik ILS, a Khrom-Nikel' IFF system, an RSIU-3 radio and an RV-2 radio altimeter. The armament still consisted of three 37-mm (1.45 calibre) Nudelman/Suranov NS-37 cannons but the cannon placement was reversed (two to port and one to starboard).

With a view to increasing range the '200BF' featured new wings which were of similar planform to the existing ones but were very different structurally, incorporating integral fuel tanks of 1,000 litres (220 Imp gal) capacity each, as well as extra hardpoints for the rockets inboard of the drop tanks. In contrast, the wings of the '200B' were largely unchanged, except for some local reinforcement to take larger and heavier drop tanks. The aircraft's internal fuel capacity was 2,810 litres (618.2 Imp gal); a further 5,300 litres (1,166 Imp gal) were carried in huge conformal (slipper) tanks.

The modifications increased the aircraft's all-up weight, with an attendant deterioration in flight performance. To compensate for this, the production version was to have the rear VK-1 engine substituted by a VK-1F after-

burning turbojet rated at 2,600 kgp (5,730 lbst) dry and 3,380 kgp (7,450 lbst) reheat, hence the F suffix signifying *s forsahzhem* (with afterburning). The interim '200B' had standard non-afterburning engines.

Speaking of weight, the Sokol radar turned out to be heavier than advertised. Hence on the planned '200BF' production version the wings were moved forward slightly to compensate for the extra weight ahead of the wing focus. On the '200B', which retained the original wings, 300 kg (660 lb) of ballast had to be installed in the rear fuselage for CG reasons.

The higher weight necessitated reinforcement of the landing gear, which had beefed-up oleos and new heavy-duty wheels. Strange as it may seem, it was the wheels that proved to be the main stumbling block preventing the flight tests from beginning on schedule. Before that, the manufacturers had already had to reinforce the tyres twice, and when asked to do this for a third time they flatly refused. Using another type of wheels was impossible because larger wheels would not fit into the existing wheel wells, and enlarging the latter obviously spelled trouble.

Eventually a solution to the wheel problem was found after all, and in June 1952 the '200B' interceptor was finally rolled out at Zhukovskiy. Manufacturer's flight tests commenced on 3rd July, with Andrey G. Kochetkov as project test pilot; the aircraft was also flown by Yakov I. Vernikov, V. N. Komarov, K. B. Makarov and A. F. Kosarev. Sure enough, the flight performance recorded in the first few test flights turned out to be lower as compared to the original aircraft; the top speed was reduced to 1,030 km/h (639 mph), the climb time to 10,000 m increased to seven minutes flat and the service ceiling decreased to 14,125 m (46,340 ft). Range on internal fuel at 10,000 m was 960 km (596 miles.

Between 27th August and 8th September 1952 the aircraft was in lay-up while reinforced landing gear struts were fitted and revisions were made to the rear engine's intake scoops in keeping with TsAGI's recommendations. A checkout flight made on 9th September showed that the maximum speed had increased by some 10 km/h (6.2 mph). Later the flights were suspended again for the purpose of integrating the unguided rockets and making a trial fit of the drop tanks; the latter were also tested for vibration resistance (fatigue strength). By then 'aircraft 200B' had logged 18 hours 28 minutes in 32 flights.

The Yak-120 patrol interceptor also entered flight test in the summer of 1952. This fighter, which had wings swept back 45° and

less thirsty engines located in underwing nacelles, was smaller and lighter, which gave it higher performance as compared to the '200B'. By November the Yakovlev fighter had largely completed its manufacturer's flight tests. Yet the aircraft was still radar-less because development of the Sokol radar was dragging considerably behind schedule; this meant the Yak-120 could not be submitted for state acceptance trials. The only way out in this situation was to equip the interceptor with the Izumrood radar as a stop-gap measure, since this was the first Soviet AI radar to pass trials with satisfactory results and be cleared for production. In early December 1952 MAP issued an order to the effect that the Yak-120 be fitted with the Izumrood radar submitted for state acceptance trials. In the meantime, 'aircraft 200B' was to be transferred to NII-17, which used it as an avionics testbed for debugging the Sokol.

Soon afterwards the '200B' was fitted with a functional Sokol radar. Manufacturer's tests

of this unit lasted throughout the first six months of 1953, with Mark L. Gallai as project test pilot. state acceptance trials of the radar on the '200B' at GK NII VVS began on 26th June. Eventually the manufacturer succeeded in ironing out the radar's main 'bugs' and simplifying its operational and maintenance procedures. All in all, the '200B' made 109 flights in the radar testbed role.

By mid-1953 the radar had reached an adequate reliability standard. Hence in November 1953 the tests of the radar on the Lavochkin interceptor were terminated and the go-ahead was given to install the radar in the Yak-120. The result was the Yak-120M, known as the Yak-25M in production form.

Thus ended one of the Soviet attempts to create an all-weather interceptor. The '200' was Lavochkin's penultimate aircraft. Later, OKB-301 built and tested the '250' (La-250) supersonic heavy interceptor, but this fared no better than the predecessor, ending Lavochkin's association with manned aviation.

Basic Specifications of the '200' and '200B'

	200 Manufacturer's flight tests	200 State acceptance trials	200B Manufacturer's flight tests	200B State acceptance trials
Crew	2	2	2	2
Powerplant	2 x VK-1	2 x VK-1	2 x VK-1	2 x VK-1
Thrust, kgp (lbst)	2 x 2,700 (2 x 5,950)	2 x 2,700 (2 x 5,950)	2 x 2,700 (2 x 5,950)	2 x 2,700 (2 x 5,950)
Radar type	Toriy-A	Toriy-A	Korshun	Sokol
Length overall	16.594 m (54 ft 5¹⁹⁄₆₄ in)	16.594 m (54 ft 5¹⁹⁄₆₄ in)	16.351 m (53 ft 7¾ in)	17.33 m (56 ft 10½₂ in)
Height on ground	4.28 m (14 ft 0½ in)	4.28 m (14 ft 0¹³⁄₃₂ in)	4.28 m (14 ft 0½ in)	5.06 m (16 ft 7⁷⁄₃₂ in)
Wing span	12.96 m (42 ft 6¹⁵⁄₆₄ in)	12.96 m (42 ft 6¹⁵⁄₆₄ in)	12.96 m (42 ft 6¹⁵⁄₆₄ in)	12.96 m (42 ft 6¹⁵⁄₆₄ in)
Wing area, m² (sq ft)	40.02 (430.32)	40.02 (430.32)	40.02 (430.32)	40.02 (430.32)
Wing sweep at quarter-chord	40°	40°	40°	40°
Empty weight, kg (lb)	n.a.	7,090 (15,630)	n.a.	8,810 (19,420)
Take-off weight, kg (lb):				
normal	9,910 (21,850) *	10,375 (22,870)	10,580 (23,325)	11,560 (25,485)
maximum (with drop tanks)	n.a.	12,375 (27,280)	12,630 (27,840)	16,244 (35,811) †
Fuel load, kg (lb):				
normal	2,400 (5,290)	2,295 (5,060)	2,554 (5,630)	2,345 (5,170)
maximum (with drop tanks)	n.a.	4,135 (9,115)	4,430 (9,770)	6,784 (14,955) ‡
Maximum speed, km/h (mph)	1,090 (677)	1,062 (659)	1,070 (664)	1,030 (639)
at altitude, m (ft)	3,500 (11,480)	4,500 (14,760)	5,000 (16,400)	5,000 (16,400)
Maximum speed at 10,000 m (32,810 ft), km/h (mph)	1,020 (633)	1,025 (636)	1,031 (640)	1,007 (625)
Maximum Mach number attained	0.946	0.986 †	0.95 †	0.95 †
Climb time to 10,000 m, minutes	5.85	6.6	6.0	7.0
Rate of climb, m/sec (ft/min)	n.a.	n.a.	27,78 (5,470)	23,81 (4,690)
Service ceiling, m (ft)	15,200 (49,870)	15,150 (49,700)	15,550 (51,020)	14,125 (46,340)
Maximum range, km (miles):				
on internal fuel	1,311 (814)	1,025 (636)	1,170 (726)	960 (596)
with drop tanks at 10,000 m	n.a.	2,000 (1,242)	2,170 (1,347)	3,000 (1,863)
Armament	3 x 37 mm cannons	3 x 37 mm cannons	3 x 37 mm cannons	3 x 37 mm cannons
Crew	2	2	2	2

* No radar

† In a shallow dive

‡ Estimated

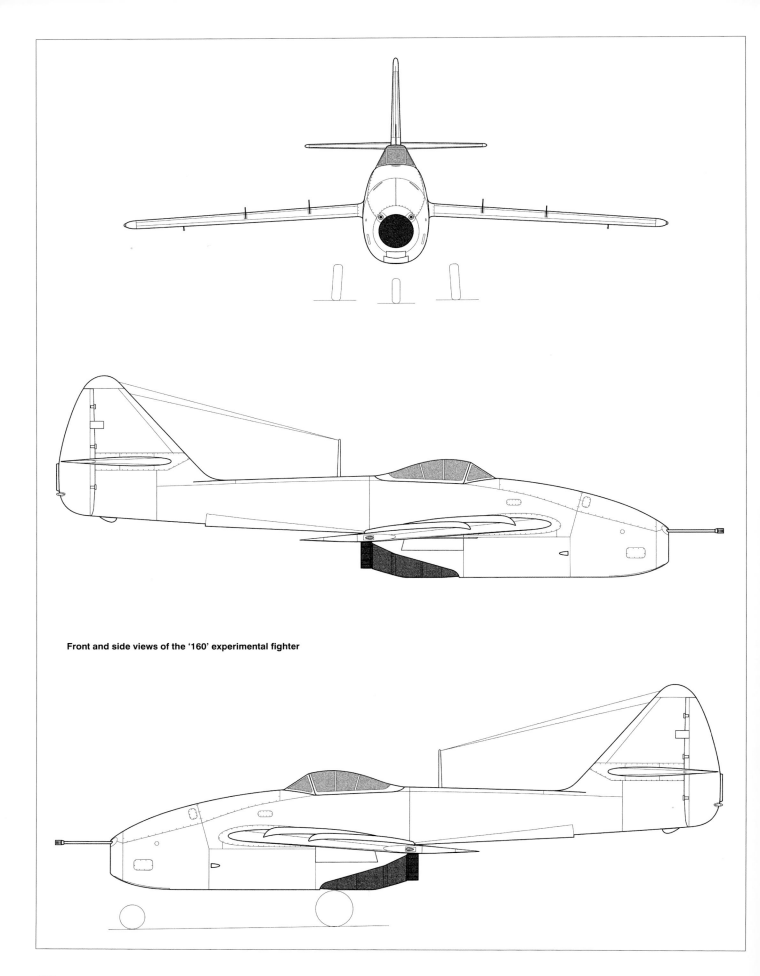

Front and side views of the '160' experimental fighter

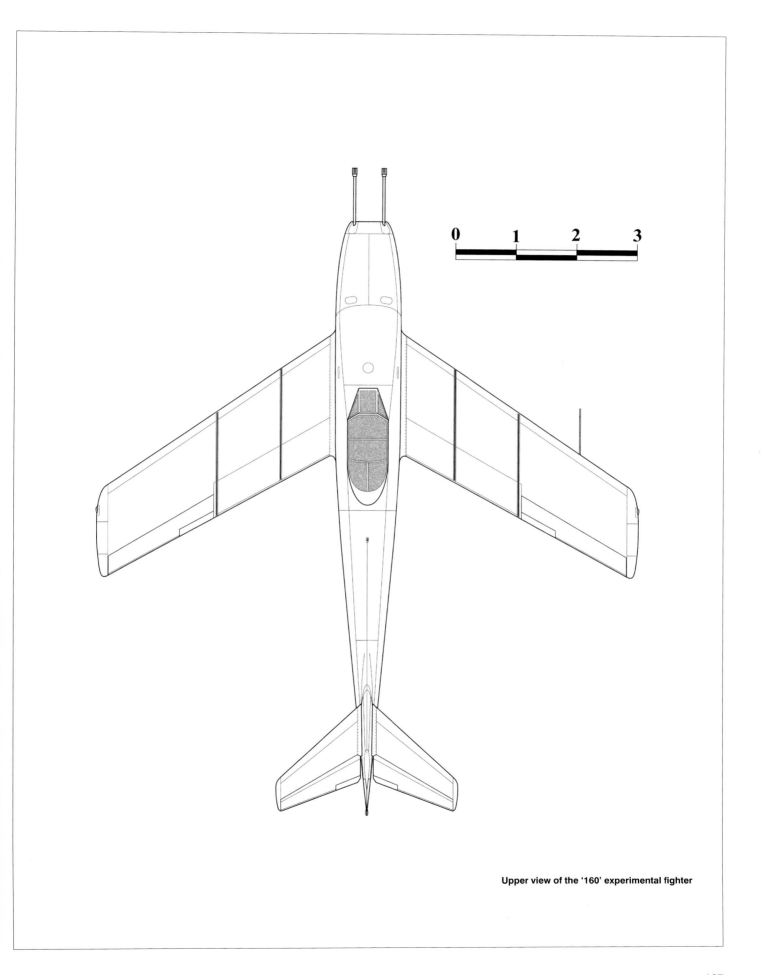

Upper view of the '160' experimental fighter

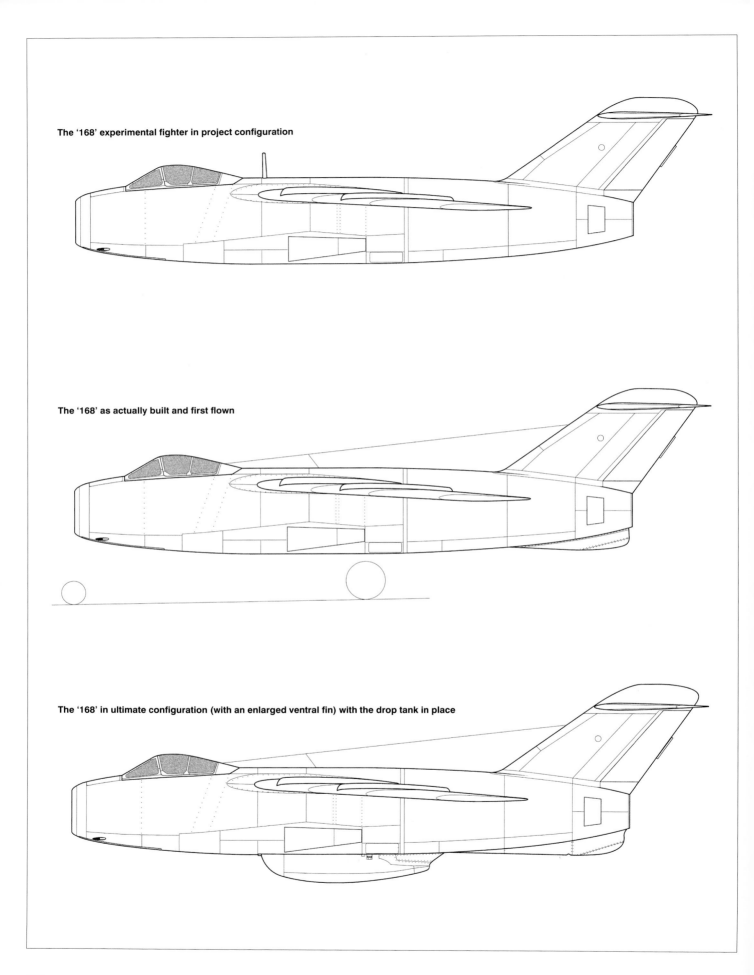

The '168' experimental fighter in project configuration

The '168' as actually built and first flown

The '168' in ultimate configuration (with an enlarged ventral fin) with the drop tank in place

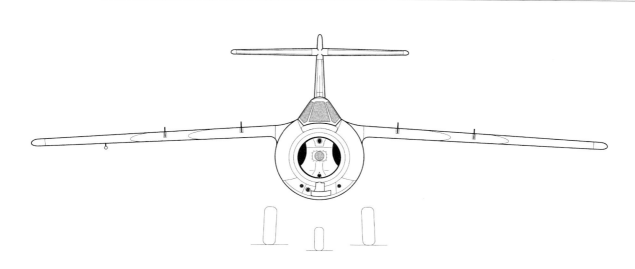

Front and upper views of the '168' experimental fighter

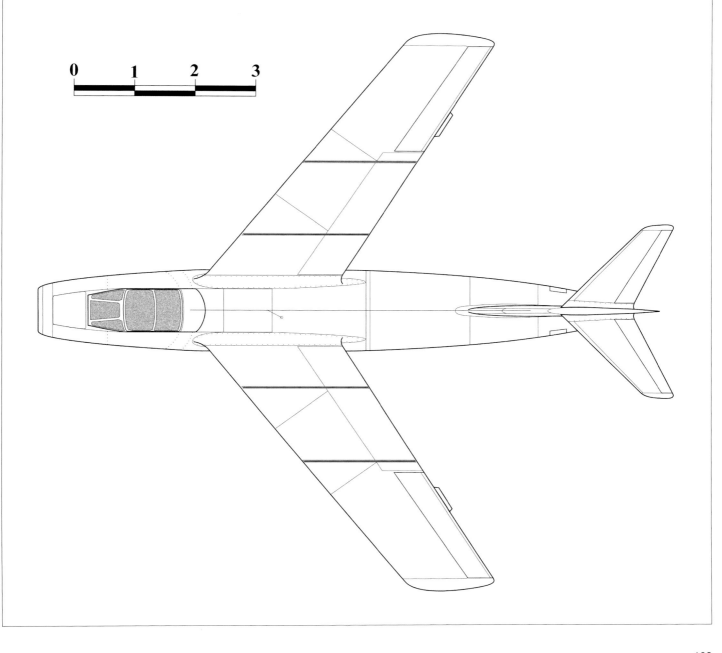

0   1   2   3

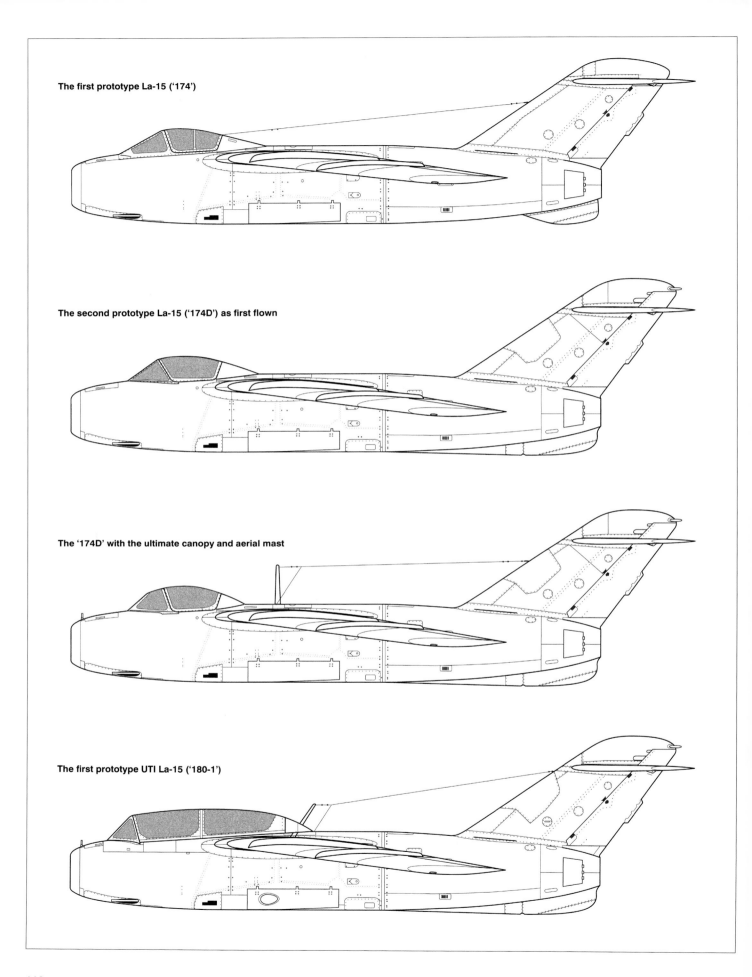

The first prototype La-15 ('174')

The second prototype La-15 ('174D') as first flown

The '174D' with the ultimate canopy and aerial mast

The first prototype UTI La-15 ('180-1')

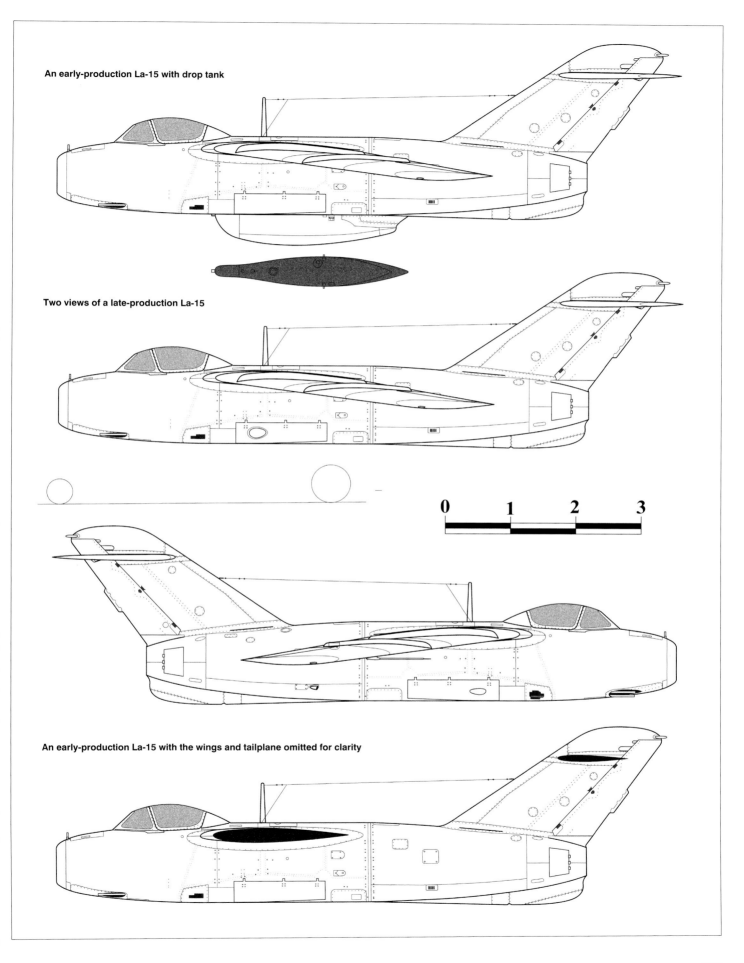

An early-production La-15 with drop tank

Two views of a late-production La-15

An early-production La-15 with the wings and tailplane omitted for clarity

0 1 2 3

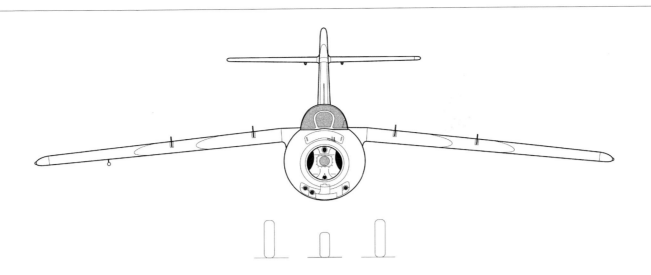

Front and lower views of an early-production La-15

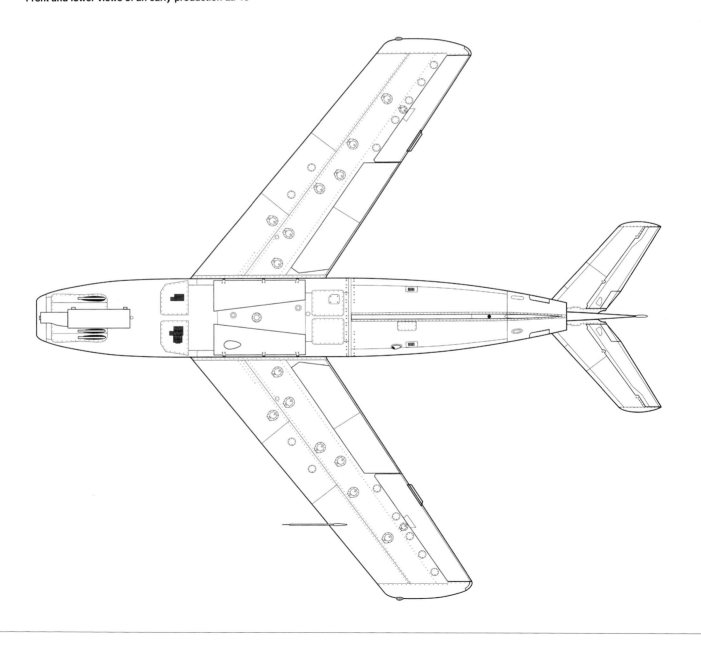

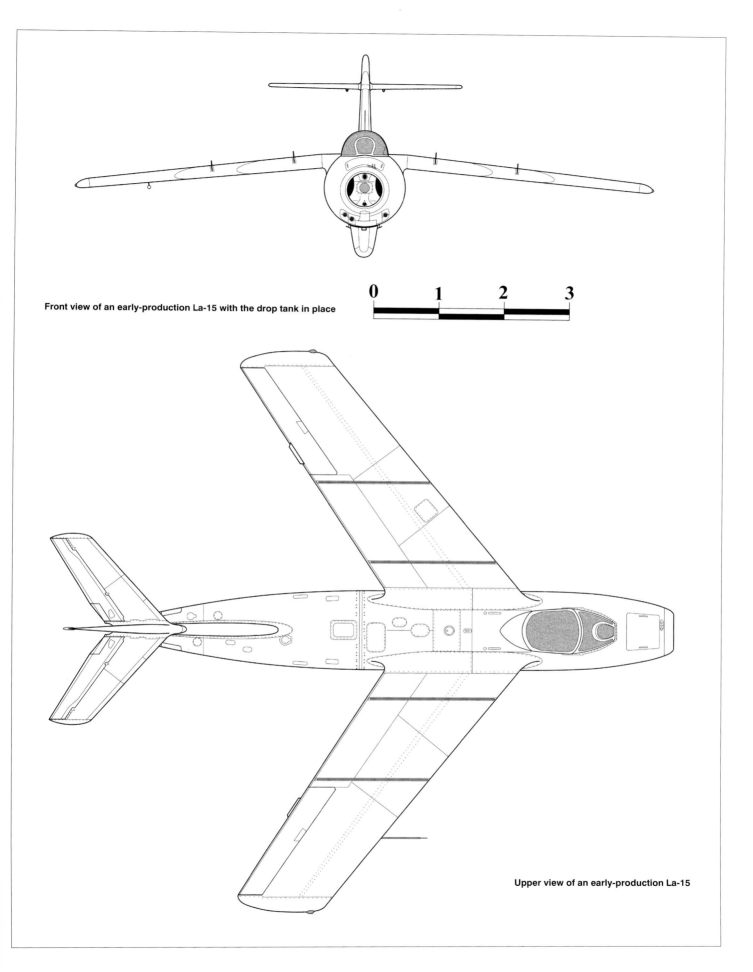

Front view of an early-production La-15 with the drop tank in place

0   1   2   3

Upper view of an early-production La-15

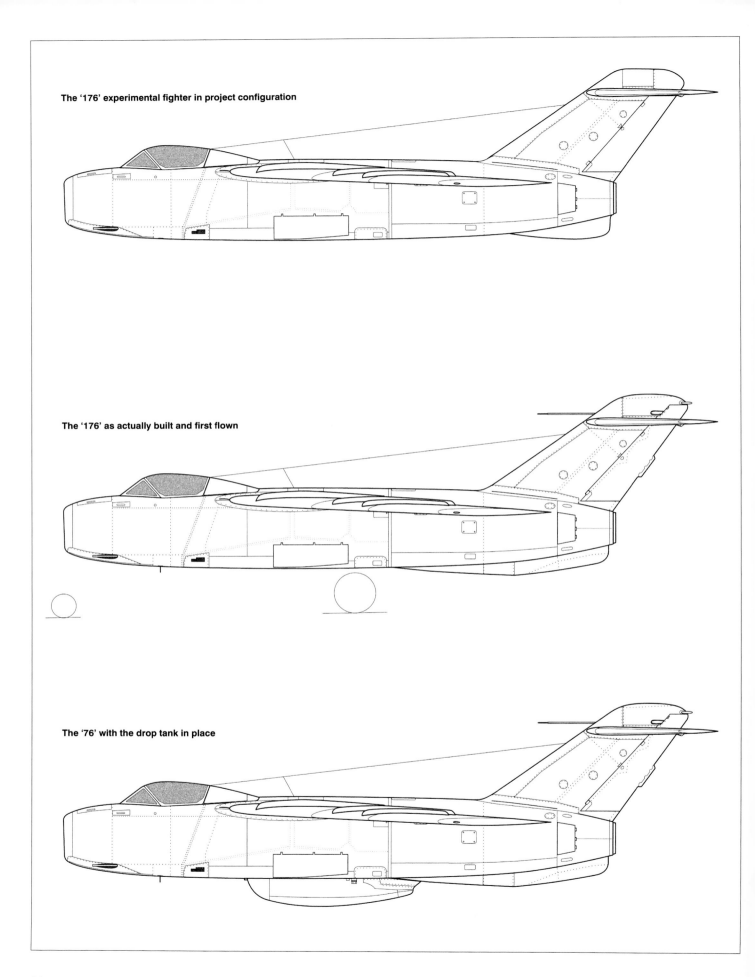

The '176' experimental fighter in project configuration

The '176' as actually built and first flown

The '76' with the drop tank in place

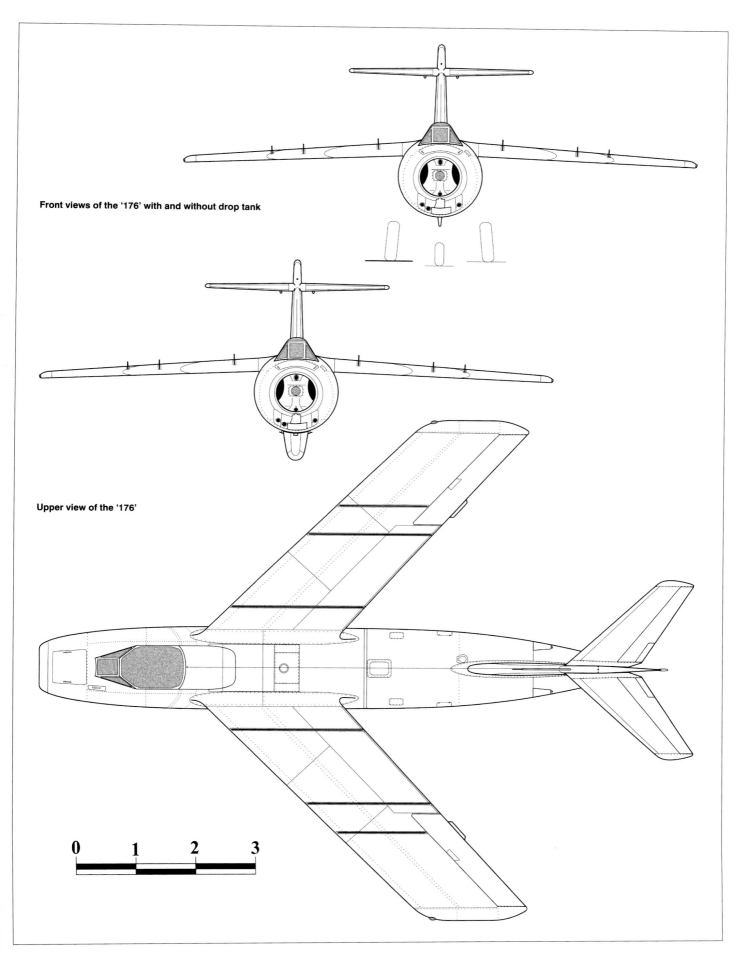

Front views of the '176' with and without drop tank

Upper view of the '176'

0   1   2   3

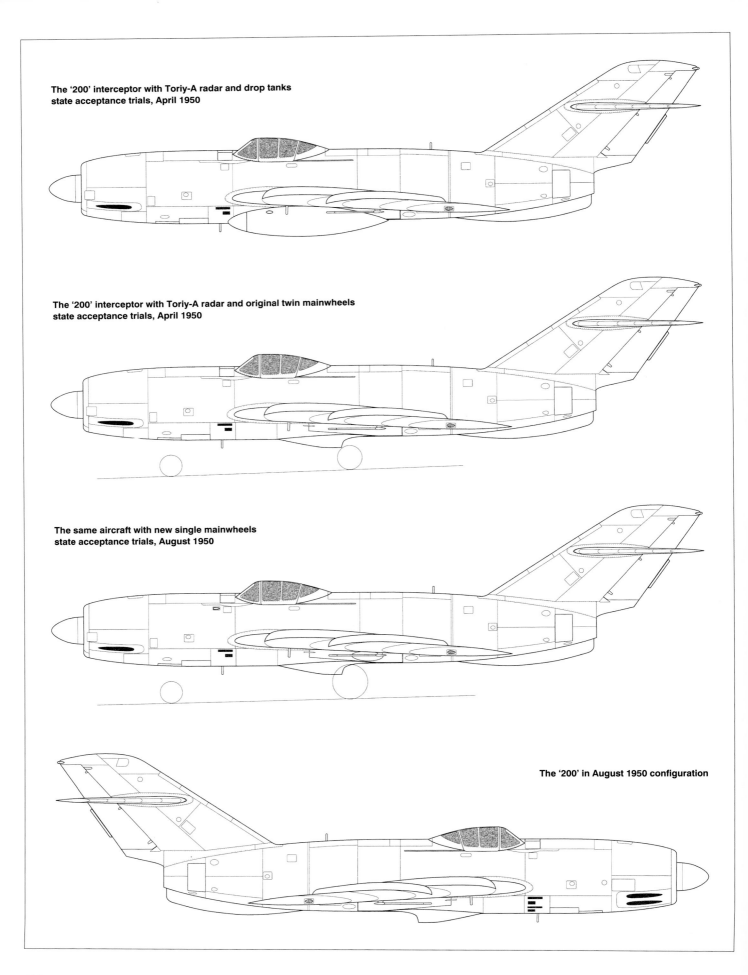

The '200' interceptor with Toriy-A radar and drop tanks
state acceptance trials, April 1950

The '200' interceptor with Toriy-A radar and original twin mainwheels
state acceptance trials, April 1950

The same aircraft with new single mainwheels
state acceptance trials, August 1950

The '200' in August 1950 configuration

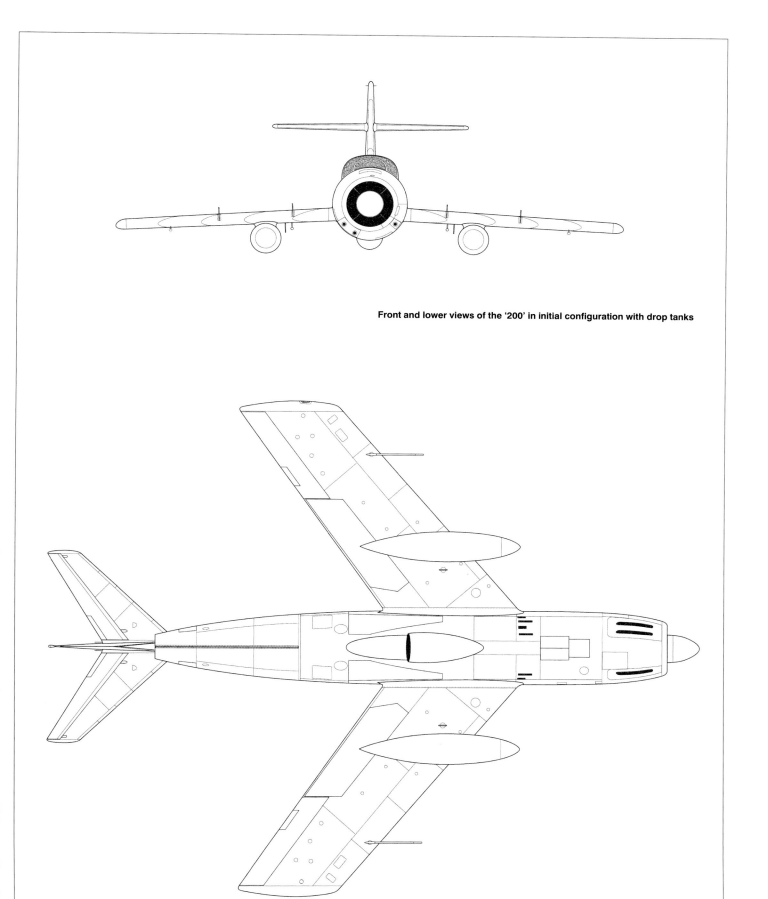

Front and lower views of the '200' in initial configuration with drop tanks

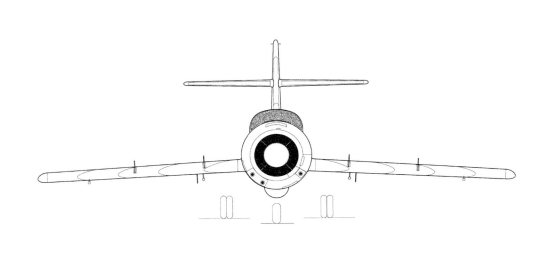

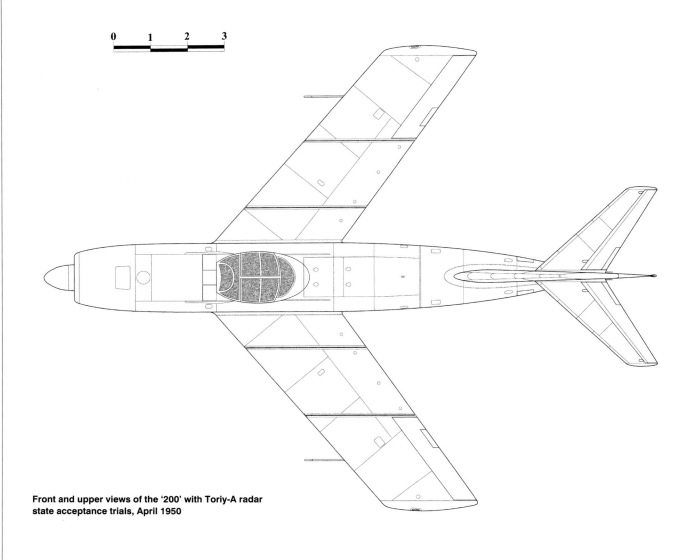

Front and upper views of the '200' with Toriy-A radar state acceptance trials, April 1950

0 1 2 3

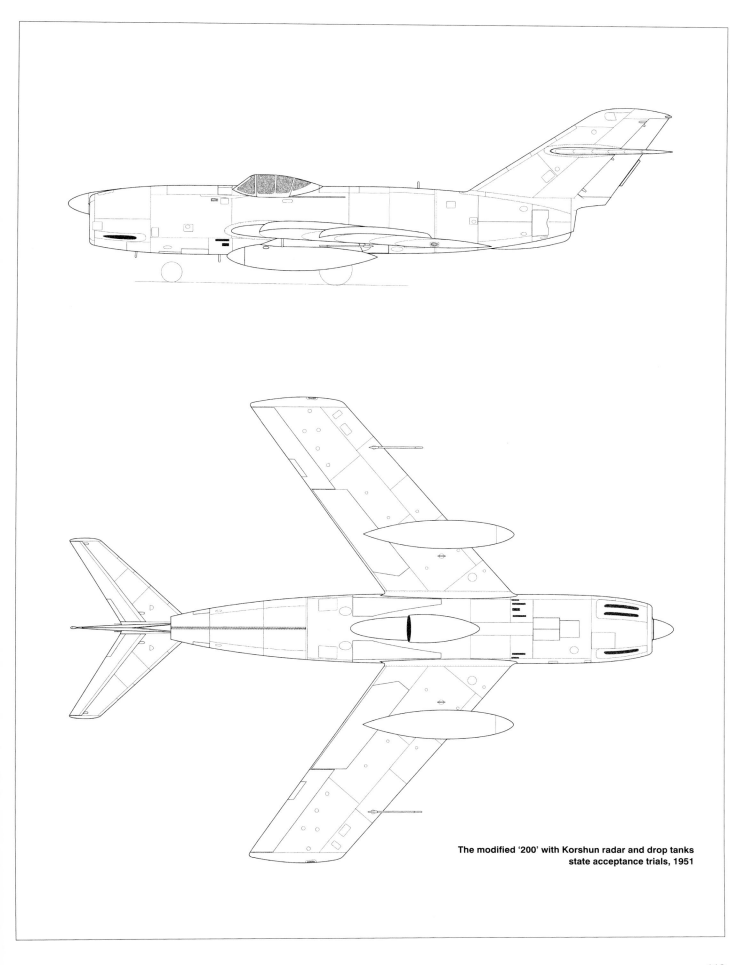

The modified '200' with Korshun radar and drop tanks
state acceptance trials, 1951

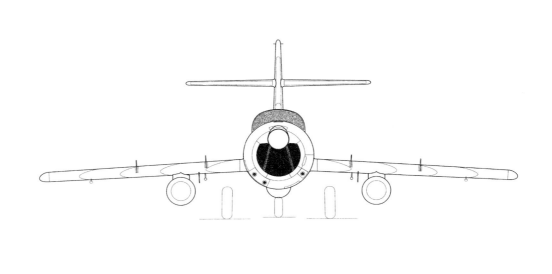

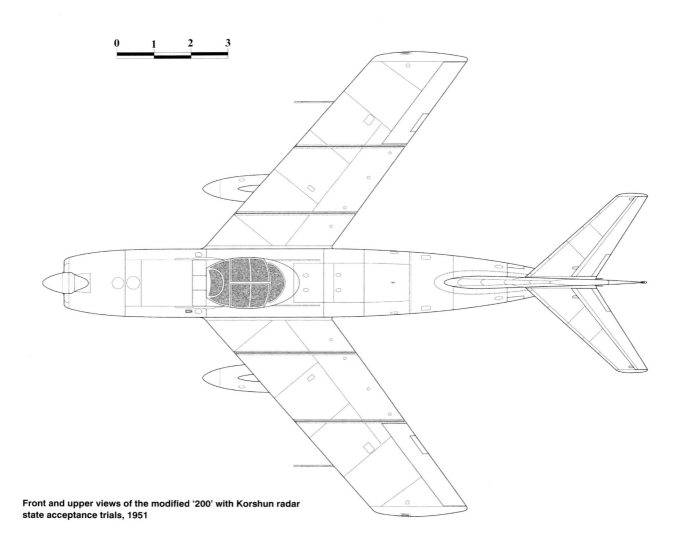

Front and upper views of the modified '200' with Korshun radar state acceptance trials, 1951

0 1 2 3

**The '200B' interceptor with Sokol radar and drop tanks
NII-1, late 1952**

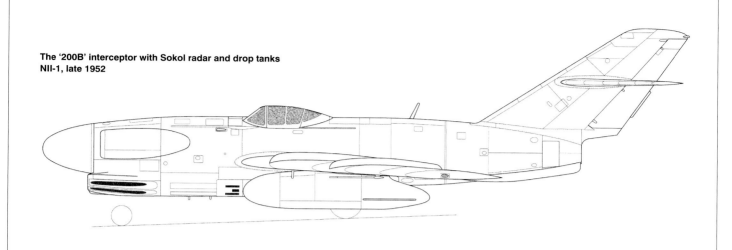

The '200B' with two ARS-212 unguided rockets

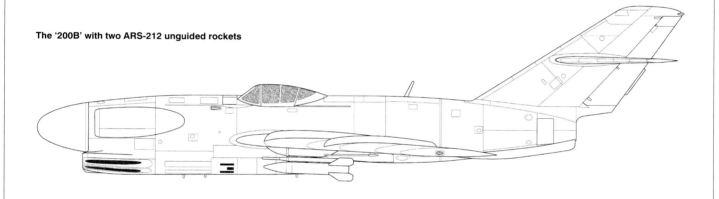

The '200B' with four TRS-190 unguided rockets in ORO-190 launch tubes

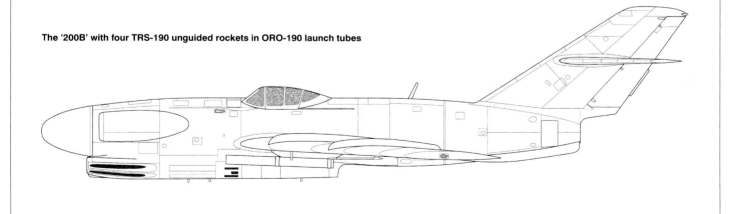

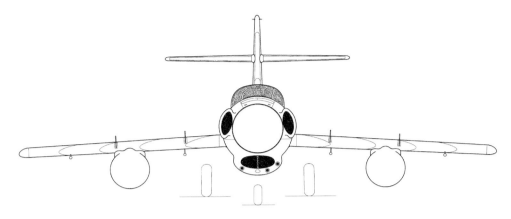

**The '200B' interceptor with drop tanks
NII-1, late 1952**

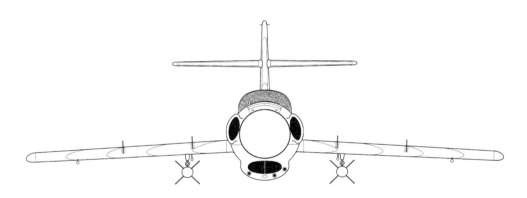

The '200B' with ARS-212 unguided rockets

The '200B' with TRS-190 unguided rockets

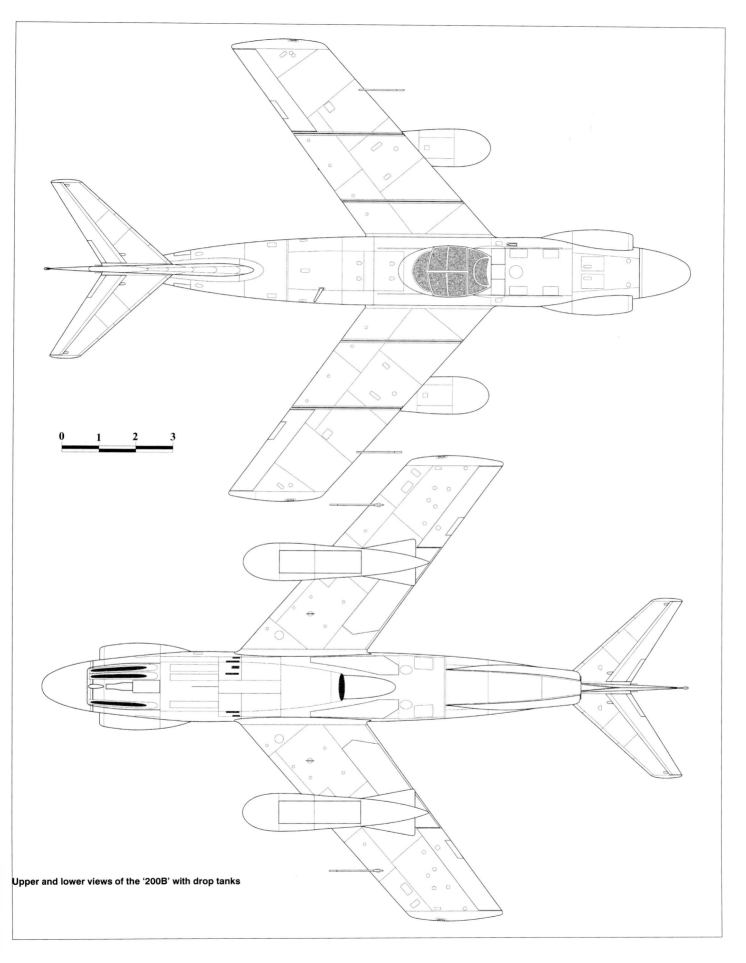

0 1 2 3

Upper and lower views of the '200B' with drop tanks

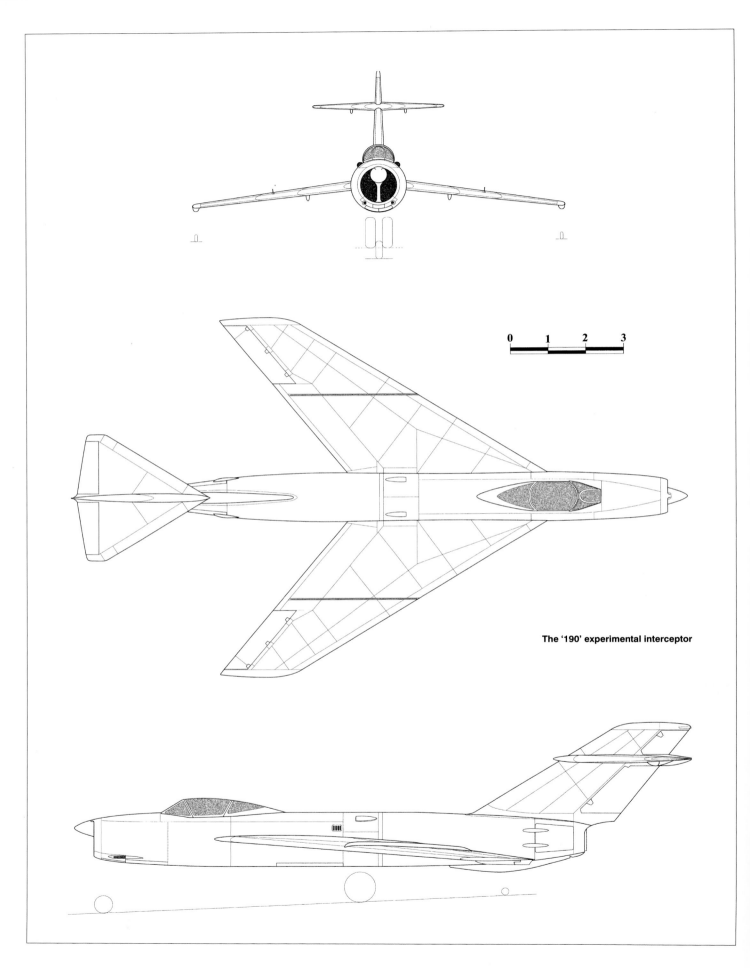

The '190' experimental interceptor

An extremely rare colour shot of a red-nosed 196th IAP La-15 ('108 White', c/n 52210108) taking off. The inset shows ten of the unit's La-15s making a formation take-off at Kubinka AB as they head east towards Moscow-Tushino for the Aviation Day parade in August 1949.
Below: Yevgeniy G. Pepelyayev performs solo aerobatics over Tushino in La-15 '228 White' (c/n 52210228).

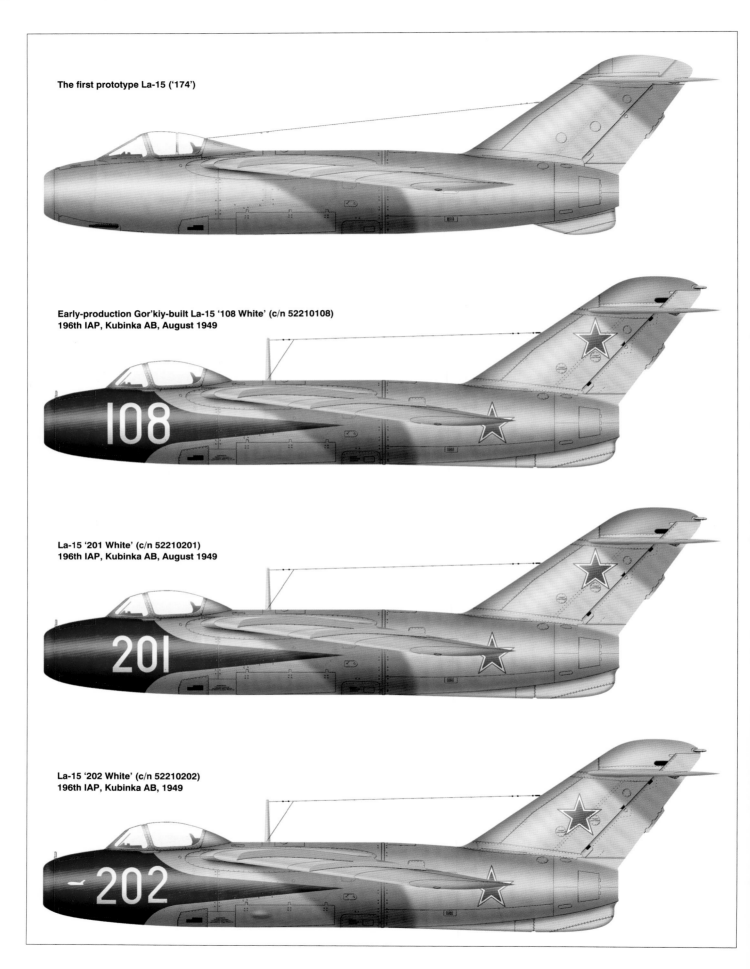

The first prototype La-15 ('174')

Early-production Gor'kiy-built La-15 '108 White' (c/n 52210108)
196th IAP, Kubinka AB, August 1949

La-15 '201 White' (c/n 52210201)
196th IAP, Kubinka AB, August 1949

La-15 '202 White' (c/n 52210202)
196th IAP, Kubinka AB, 1949

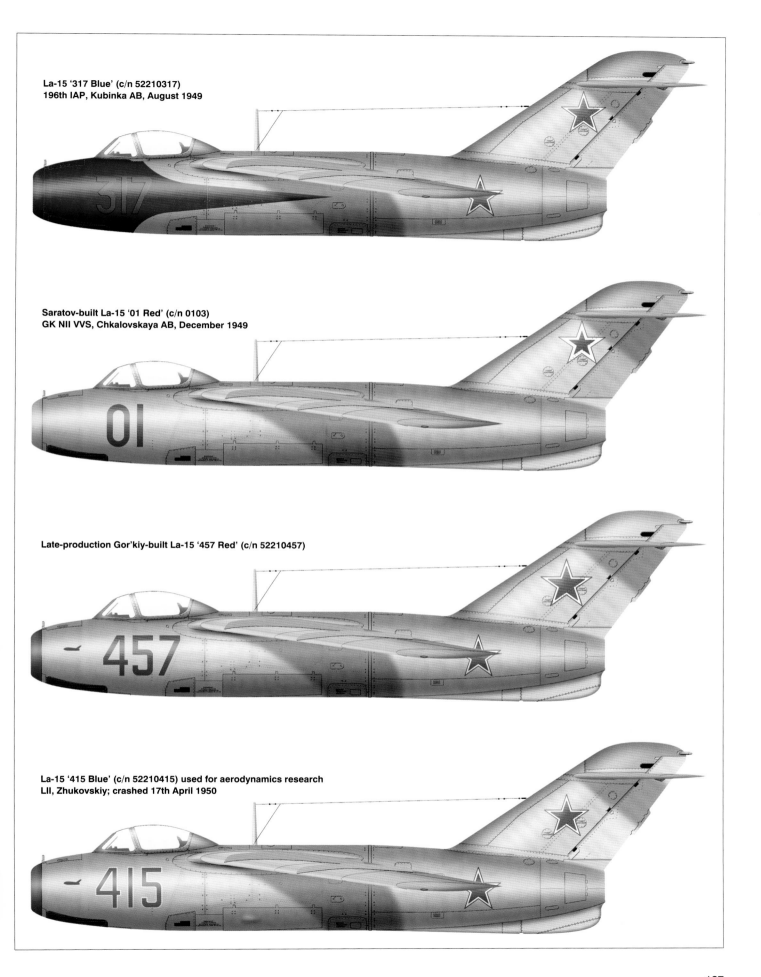

La-15 '317 Blue' (c/n 52210317)
196th IAP, Kubinka AB, August 1949

Saratov-built La-15 '01 Red' (c/n 0103)
GK NII VVS, Chkalovskaya AB, December 1949

Late-production Gor'kiy-built La-15 '457 Red' (c/n 52210457)

La-15 '415 Blue' (c/n 52210415) used for aerodynamics research
LII, Zhukovskiy; crashed 17th April 1950

We hope you enjoyed this book . . .

Midland Publishing titles are edited and designed by an experienced and enthusiastic team of specialists.

We always welcome ideas from authors or readers for books they would like to see published.

In addition, our associate, Midland Counties Publications, offers an exceptionally wide range of aviation, military, naval and transport books and DVDs for sale by mail-order worldwide.

For a copy of the appropriate catalogue, or to order further copies of this book, and any other Midland Publishing titles, please write, telephone, fax or e-mail to:

Midland Counties Publications
4 Watling Drive, Hinckley,
Leics, LE10 3EY, England
Tel: (+44) 01455 254 450
Fax: (+44) 01455 233 737
E-mail: midlandbooks@compuserve.com
www.midlandcountiessuperstore.com

US distribution by Specialty Press –
see page 2.

Earlier titles in the series:

Vols 1, 3 to 15 are still available
Vol.16: Sukhoi Interceptors
Vol.17: Early Soviet Jet Bombers
Vol.18: Antonov's Heavy Transports
Vol.19: Soviet Heavy Interceptors
Vol.20: Soviet/Russian UAVs
Vol.21: Antonov's Jet Twins
Vol.22: Mil's Heavylift Helicopters
Vol.23: Soviet/Russian AWACS Aircraft
Vol.24: Tupolev Tu-144

Red Star Volume 25
ILYUSHIN IL-12 & IL-14
Successors to the Li-2

Yefim Gordon and Dmitry Komissarov

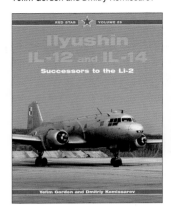

Designed to supersede the Li-2, the 29-seat IL-12 airliner entered Aeroflot service in 1948. Some 600 were built for Aeroflot and the Soviet armed forces. The improved IL-14 entered production in 1953, the type was exported to China, Bulgaria, Romania and Poland as well as being built by VEB in East Germany and Asia in Czechoslovakia. The total production of over 1,000 aircraft included 203 Avia 14s and Avia 14 Supers – the latter being a pressurised development.

Softback, 280 x 215 mm, 128 pages
180 b/w photos, 16 pages of colour
plus 12 pages of drawings
978 1 85780 223 8 **£19.99**

Red Star Volume 26
RUSSIA'S MILITARY AIRCRAFT IN THE 21st CENTURY

Yefim Gordon

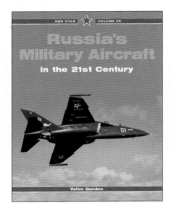

While the large new aircraft programmes of the Cold War era are a thing of the past, military aviation in Russia is not standing still. This volume looks at programmes like the new Mi-8MTKO and Mi-24PN night-capable helicopters, the latest Sukhoi upgrades such as the Su-24M2, Su-25SM and Su-27SM, new and more capable missiles for the Tu-95MS and Tu-160 bombers and the revamping of the training fleet with the Yak-130.

Softback, 280 x 215 mm, 128 pages
269 full colour photographs,
plus line drawings
978 1 85780 224 5 **£19.99**

Red Star Volume 27
LISUNOV Li-2
The Soviet DC-3

Y Gordon, S and D Komissarov

When they bought a manufacturing licence for the DC-3 in 1936, Soviet decision makers had no way of knowing the place the Douglas airliner would come to occupy in aviation's hall of fame. Adapted to employ Russian engines and materials, the DC-3 entered production as the PS-84; later redesignated Li-2. This addition to the series explores what is probably the least-known aspect of the history of one of the world's best-known airliners.

Softback, 280 x 215 mm, 128 pages
235 b/w photographs, plus
12 pages of colour
978 1 85780 228 3 **£19.99**

Red Star Volume 28
BERIEV'S JET FLYING BOATS

Yefim Gordon, Andrey Sal'nikov and Aleksandr Zablotskiy

Established during the 1930s, Beriev is one of the less well known of the Soviet design bureaus. Their forte lay in the development of flying boats. Whilst these have been powered by both piston and jet engines, this book focuses on those jet-engined aircraft produced from the late 1960s onwards, including the Be-10, A-40 and Be-200. These aircraft were intended for a variety of roles, such as passenger transport and maritime rescue operations.

Softback, 280 x 215 mm, 128 pages
206 b/w photos, 16 pages of colour,
plus 12 pages of drawings
978 1 85780 236 8 **£19.99**

Red Star Volume 29
KAMOV -27/-32 FAMILY

Yefim Gordon and Dmitriy Komissarov

An in-depth study of this family of helicopter designs with their distinctive contra-rotating rotors. The Kamov Ka-27 helicopter was first produced for the Soviet navy in 1973. Several variants including the Ka-29 and Ka-31, were later built. This aircraft was followed in 1980 by a civilian version, the Ka-32. This was in turn followed by several variants including those for transport and shipboard utility purposes.

Softback, 280 x 215 mm, 128 pages
230 b/w photos, 22 pages of colour,
plus line drawings
978 1 85780 237 5 **£19.99**

Red Star Volume 30
SOVIET ROCKET FIGHTERS

Yefim Gordon

Fighter designers had always tried to make their aircraft go faster. To achieve this some Soviet designers used liquid-propellant rocket motors. The first attempt was the BI, which made its first powered flight on 15th May 1942. Projects from Polikarpov and Mikoyan, the latter based on captured German research, followed before Iliya F Florov's 4302 programme was cancelled at the end of 1947 in favour of turbojet-powered fighters.

Softback, 280 x 215 mm, 128 pages
257 black/white photographs,
plus 54 drawings
978 1 85780 245 0 **£19.99**

Red Star Volume 31
TUPOLEV Tu-114

Yefim Gordon and Vladimir Rigmant

Based upon the earlier Tu-95 strategic bomber, the Tu-114 was the largest airliner constructed to that time. It carried up to 220 passengers at speeds approaching those of a jet; the speed record it set for turbo-prop aircraft still stands today. Aeroflot employed a fleet of 31 on its long-range domestic and international routes, the last being withdrawn in 1975. Some examples were later converted as Tu-126 'Moss' AWACS aircraft for the Soviet Navy.

Softback, 280 x 215 mm, 128 pages
194 b/w, 51 colour photographs,
plus 11 drawings
978 1 85780 246 7 **£19.99**